W9-DEJ-900

AMERICAN
WAR LIBRARY

★ ★ ★ ★

★ **The Persian Gulf War** ★

# LEADERS AND
# GENERALS

Titles in The American War Library series include:

**World War II**
Hitler and the Nazis
Kamikazes
Leaders and Generals
Life as a POW
Life of an American Soldier in
  Europe
Strategic Battles in Europe
Strategic Battles in the Pacific
The War at Home
Weapons of War

**The Civil War**
Leaders of the North and South
Life Among the Soldiers and
  Cavalry
Lincoln and the Abolition of
  Slavery

Strategic Battles
Weapons of War

**The Persian Gulf War**
Leaders and Generals
Life of an American Soldier
The War Against Iraq
Weapons of War

**The Vietnam War**
A History of U.S. Involvement
The Home Front: Americans
  Protest the War
Leaders and Generals
Life as a POW
Life of an American Soldier
Weapons of War

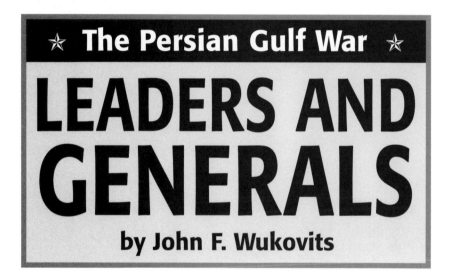

★ The Persian Gulf War ★

# LEADERS AND GENERALS

by John F. Wukovits

Lucent Books, P.O. Box 289011, San Diego, CA 92198-9011

Library of Congress Cataloging-in-Publication Data

Wukovits, John F., 1944–
    Leaders and Generals / by John F. Wukovits.
       p. cm.—(The American war library series. Persian Gulf War)
    Includes bibliographical references and index.
    ISBN 1-56006-714-4 (alk. paper)
    1. Persian Gulf War, 1991—Biography—Juvenile literature.
    [1. Persian Gulf War, 1991—Biography. 2. Generals.] I. Title. II. Series.
    DS79.723 .W85 2001
    956.7044'2'0922—dc21

                                00-010097

19.95

# ★ Contents ★

# A Nation Forged by War

The United States, like many nations, was forged and defined by war. Despite Benjamin Franklin's opinion that "There never was a good war or a bad peace," the United States owes its very existence to the War of Independence, one to which Franklin wholeheartedly subscribed. The country forged by war in 1776 was tempered and made stronger by the Civil War in the 1860s.

The Texas Revolution, the Mexican-American War, and the Spanish-American War expanded the country's borders and gave it overseas possessions. These wars made the United States a world power, but this status came with a price, as the nation became a key but reluctant player in both World War I and World War II.

Each successive war further defined the country's role on the world stage. Following World War II, U.S. foreign policy redefined itself to focus on the role of defender, not only of the freedom of its own citizens, but also of the freedom of people everywhere. During the cold war that followed World War II until the collapse of the Soviet Union, defending the world meant fighting communism. This goal, manifested in the Korean and Vietnam conflicts, proved elusive, and soured the American public on its achievability. As the United States emerged as the world's sole superpower, American foreign policy has been guided less by national interest and more on protecting international human rights. But as involvement in Somalia and Kosovo prove, this goal has been equally elusive.

As a result, the country's view of itself changed. Bolstered by victories in World Wars I and II, Americans first relished the role of protector. But, as war followed war in a seemingly endless procession, Americans began to doubt their leaders, their motives, and themselves. The Vietnam War especially caused people to question the validity of sending its young people to die in places where they were not particularly wanted and for people who did not seem especially grateful.

While the most obvious changes brought about by America's wars have been geopolitical in nature, many other aspects of society have been touched. War often does not bring about change directly, but acts instead like the catalyst in a chemical reaction, accelerating changes already in progress.

Some of these changes have been societal. The role of women in the United States had been slowly changing, but World War II put thousands into the workforce and into uniform. They might have gone back to being housewives after the war, but equality, once experienced, would not be forgotten.

Likewise, wars have accelerated technological change. The necessity for faster airplanes and a more destructive bomb led to the development of jet planes and nuclear energy. Artificial fibers developed for parachutes in the 1940s were used in the clothing of the 1950s.

Lucent Books' American War Library covers key wars in the development of the nation. Each war is covered in several volumes, to allow for more detail, context, and to provide volumes on often neglected subjects, such as the kamikazes of World War II, or weapons used in the Civil War. As with all Lucent Books, notes, annotated bibliographies, and appendixes such as glossaries give students a launching point for further research. In addition, sidebars and archival photographs enhance the text. Together, each volume in The American War Library will aid students in understanding how America's wars have shaped and changed its politics, economics, and society.

# A Common Strain

Every war throughout history bears the names of famous commanders who led their soldiers to victory. Sometimes it was the leader of the nation, such as Alexander the Great, who guided his Greek phalanxes to triumph after triumph as they swept across Asia and North Africa. On other occasions it was the commander of a division or company.

In any event, these individuals succeeded because of the distinctive leadership they brought to the battle. Alexander chose to command his men through example, and thus he was often found fighting in the front lines with his troops. In the American Civil War, the South's "Stonewall" Jackson rallied his soldiers at Manassas Junction by calmly riding back and forth in plain sight and cautioning them to remain steady, while the North's Ulysses S. Grant vanquished his foe by assembling an overpowering conglomeration of men and supplies.

World War II gave us Brig. Gen. Anthony McAuliffe, whose stirring reply of "Nuts" to a German surrender ultimatum during the 1944 Battle of the Bulge reinvigorated his surrounded men and contributed to their survival until help arrived. One man who hastened to McAuliffe's relief, Gen. George S. Patton, infused discipline in his men and fear in his enemy with a deft combination of skilled military strategy, absolute confidence, and a colorful array of quotes.

In every instance, the soldiers fighting on the battlefield took their cue from the officers and leaders above them. Greek fighters took heart in seeing their commander wielding a sword and stepping into battle at their side. Patton's men may have detested his arrogance and insistence on soldierly discipline, but they loved his results and thus fought hard for the man. McAuliffe's cold, weary soldiers may have felt like giving up, but they battled on with renewed spirit after they learned of his response to the Germans.

What makes leaders in the Persian Gulf War distinctive? Did they share traits

*World War II general George S. Patton (top) and Ulysses S. Grant (bottom), commander of the Union forces during the Civil War.*

mon strains tie together the men found in this book.

During the Persian Gulf War, American political and military leaders developed a clearly stated set of goals for which the men and women of the United States fought. From President George H. W. Bush down to the lowest officer, every soldier knew that the United States and its coalition allies were braving the rigors of the Mideast desert to force Saddam Hussein's Iraqi army out of Kuwait and to destroy his capability to wage war in the future. Citizens back home understood the same. Fighting for a noble cause, whether it be against "taxation without representation" or to free the Kuwaiti people, unites a nation behind its leaders.

On the other side, Hussein gained support in Iraq by emphasizing that "foreign" elements were trying to stop Iraq from obtaining what was rightfully theirs. The Mideast was an Arab land, claimed Hussein, and its natural resources belonged with them. Instead, American president George Bush wanted to control the flow of oil for his nation's benefit, not for the good of the Mideast. Hussein compared the Americans to the detested British, who had long occupied their land, and linked them to the even more despised Jewish state in Israel, which Hussein believed was a nation illegally carved from Arab land.

Secondly, the American and coalition commanders took firm action once a decision to go to war had been made. Half-hearted efforts or uncoordinated thrusts

with the above-named predecessors, or did they develop new talents of their own? Though it is dangerous to group together such diverse leaders and claim they provide similar examples, a handful of com-

were unusual in Kuwait; all-out attacks by supremely equipped forces were the norm. This resulted in a speedy victory that kept casualties to a minimum.

Hussein stumbled because he lacked such determination. His military was plagued by indecision and lack of organization. Consequently, when coalition forces rumbled into Kuwait, the Iraqi army had no appropriate military response ready.

More than in most previous wars in their nation's history, American Persian Gulf leaders learned from the past. Except for Dick Cheney, each had been a soldier in either World War II or Vietnam and so brought firsthand experience of war to the conflict. This made them more aware of the risks faced by the common soldier and affected their decisions. Because of their lack of such experience, Saddam Hussein and Tariq Aziz failed to grasp the thinking of their field commanders and army. The Iraqi leaders created reasons behind which their population could rally—to rid Arab lands of non-Arab influence and to obtain what was rightfully theirs—but they failed to solidify an equal determination in their military forces. This contributed to a poor showing on the battlefield by the Iraqi army, thousands of surrenders, and a quick end to the war.

Finally, American leaders in the Persian Gulf War showed an unbridled confidence, not only in themselves and in the righteousness of their cause, but in the ability of the American soldier to get the job done. One journalist in the 1940s, writing about President Franklin D. Roosevelt's

*U.S. president George Bush emphasized that Americans were fighting the Persian Gulf War to free Kuwait from Iraqi aggression.*

*Saddam Hussein invaded Kuwait to claim what he believed belonged to the Iraqi people.*

leadership during World War II, concluded, "His most outstanding characteristic is an air of supreme self-confidence. He always gives the impression that to him nothing is impossible, that everything will turn out all right."[1] American leaders in the Persian Gulf War followed Roosevelt's example.

For these reasons, American leaders excelled. Because their goals were less de-fined, Iraqi leaders performed poorly. Hussein's aggressive moves against Kuwait brought worldwide condemnation and international military action against him. His people paid the price for his actions.

# Chapter 1

# George Bush: Commander in Chief

**T**he top military commander in the United States never steps foot on a battlefield. Instead, he remains far from the fighting, giving overall direction to what subordinates carry out. During the Gulf War, the United States possessed a commander in chief who not only understood the military and war but had seen combat at close hand. In addition, his many years in politics enabled him to look at the complete picture rather than view it exclusively from the battlefield perspective. Because of his experience, President George H. W. Bush brought an ideal combination to the Gulf War, a leader who permitted the military to do its job but knew when to assert his authority.

## Early Life

George Herbert Walker Bush was born on June 12, 1924, in Milton, Massachusetts, to Prescott Sheldon and Dorothy Walker Bush. Before he was one year old, the family moved closer to New York City where his father worked as an influential investment banker. Young George Bush grew up in the affluent city of Greenwich, Connecticut, with sister Nancy and brothers Prescott Jr., Jonathan, and William. George spent much of his time with his brother, Prescott Jr., who was only two years older than he. They not only shared the same bedroom but idled after school hours and summer breaks with the same friends.

George's parents provided strong guidance. His future wife, Barbara, wrote years later, "His father had enormous influence on him, and his mother had ten times more."[2] From his mother he received a driving competitiveness tempered with the ability to get along with people, while his father, an important Wall Street business executive and U.S. senator from Connecticut, imparted honesty, hard work, and a spirit of sharing. George so closely followed the dictate about sharing that he gained the nickname, "Have Half," from family members.

George felt closer to his mother than he did to his father, who bore himself with such a rigid demeanor that George, according to family friends, sometimes seemed frightened of him. The father ex-

*George Bush was strongly influenced by his parents, who instilled in him a competitive drive and the importance of sharing.*

pected every male to wear a coat and tie to dinner, and he preferred children to melt into the background. In spite of this attitude, George Bush respected his father and frequently proclaimed his love for him.

To instill a competitive drive, Prescott and Dorothy organized a continuous stream of contests and games for their children. Family members did not simply "play" card games or tiddlywinks—they instead entered Parcheesi or tiddlywinks championships. The parents even posted what was called "The Rankings," on which the children's names were placed along with how well they performed at different activities.

George's grandfather, George Herbert Walker, also provided him with guidance. One time young George took out a sailboat with his brother Prescott, when a storm suddenly blew in. Although frightened, George managed to steady the craft and return safely to shore, where he earned the praise of his grandfather. "Grandfather said he knew we could do it," said Bush later. "That gave me confidence that's lasted all my life."[3]

George's large home in Greenwich swarmed with school friends during the school year, while the family retreat at Kennebunkport, Maine, vibrated with activity all summer long. Tennis, golf, baseball, and basketball filled the moments when the youngsters were not out roaming the surrounding areas, and George excelled at them all, especially those that demanded quick moves and eye–hand coordination. George lived an idyllic youth, with caring parents and few burdens other than the normal child-hood chores. He swam, hiked in the woods, fished, and enjoyed being a child.

Even when he was president, George Bush returned to Kennebunkport to relax in the same fashion he did as a child. He confided to the press one time during a stay at the family retreat while he was presi-dent that "I'll play a good deal of golf here, a good deal of tennis, a good deal of horse-shoes, a good deal of fishing, a good deal of running—and some reading."[4]

George's education matched his up-bringing. He attended Greenwich Country Day School, where he wore those uniforms so unique to New England preparatory schools and studied a curriculum steeped in Latin and the classics. After finishing at Greenwich, Bush entered the prestigious Phillips Academy at Andover, Massachu-setts, a school bearing roots dating back to the American Revolution and boasting graduates such as actor Jack Lemmon.

While he compiled an uninspiring edu-cational record—one of his English teach-ers said that George's grades "were not very good. My remaining impression is that he just sat in the class and handed in his pa-pers"[5]—George's athletic prowess made him one of the most valuable students at Phillips. He played soccer and captained the baseball team his senior year, when he was also voted the class president. He had plans to study at Yale University immediately afterward, but events intervened. The Germans in Europe and the Japanese in the Pacific dragged the world into World War II.

## World War II

Bush graduated from Phillips in June 1942, then enlisted in the navy on his eighteenth birthday, even though he had been ac-cepted at Yale. When he completed flight training at the naval air station in Corpus Christi, Texas, and received his wings as a pilot, Bush became the youngest aviator in the navy.

In late 1943 Bush received orders to the aircraft carrier, *San Jacinto*, as a member of Torpedo Bomber Squadron VT51. Bush pi-loted the aircraft on its bombing runs, while two gunners manned machine guns and launched the bombs. Bush nicknamed the aircraft "Barbie" after a girl he had met in the United States, Barbara Pierce.

Bush saw action right away. During one mission in the Pacific, Japanese antiaircraft fire damaged the plane's oil system and forced Bush to land in the sea. All three squadron members were quickly rescued by an American destroyer.

Bush's aircraft was again hit by enemy fire on September 2, 1944, as he flew a mis-sion against a radio shack on the island of Chichi Jima. In spite of the damage, Bush maintained enough control to complete

## Bush Joins The Navy

Like many young men his age, Bush was eager to join the fighting in World War II. He wrote of it in his book, *All the Best, George Bush.*

When Japan bombed Pearl Harbor on December 7, 1941, I was a seventeen-year-old high school senior at Phillips Academy, Andover. I could hardly wait to get out of school and enlist. Six months later, Secretary of War Henry Stimson delivered our commencement address and advised my class to go to college. He predicted it would be a long war, and there would be plenty of time for us to serve. My dad, Prescott Bush, with whom it was not easy to disagree, hoped I would listen to Secretary Stimson and go on to Yale. After the ceremony, Dad asked me if I had changed my mind. I told him no, I was "joining up." Dad simply nodded his okay. On my eighteenth birthday, June 12, 1942, I enlisted in the Navy's flight training program as a seaman second class."

*Bush served as a navy pilot during World War II.*

his bombing run, then swerved to open sea so he and the gunners could parachute to safety. One gunner jumped from the burning aircraft, but his parachute failed to open and he plunged to his death. Bush never again saw the second gunner, who most likely went down with the craft.

Bush dropped to the ocean below, then watched as fellow aviators strafed and turned back Japanese craft that sped out to capture him. They radioed Bush's location to headquarters, which dispatched a submarine to retrieve the aviator.

Bush claims that his war experience, which included fifty-eight combat missions and a Distinguished Flying Cross, helped prepare him for his future in politics. Since he observed both the values and horrors of war firsthand, he understood that sometimes military force is necessary but realized it should be used only as a final resort.

### Business and Politics

Bush returned home in December 1944 to train new pilots near Norfolk, Virginia. He also finalized a personal matter by marrying Barbara Pierce, the girl he had met before heading to the Pacific and had described to his mother as "too cute for words—really beautiful."[6] On January 6,

1945, he wed the Smith College student in Rye, New York.

After the war ended, Bush attended Yale University, where he received a B.A. in economics in only three years and gained admittance to Phi Beta Kappa, an organization consisting of the top students in the nation. He impressed people outside of the classroom as well, captaining the varsity baseball team in his senior year into the finals of the National Collegiate Athletic Association championships and participating in community service projects near Yale University. Bush was also accepted into the exclusive Skull and Bones campus society, a small fraternity-style organization that enrolled new members based on wealth and connections and insisted on secrecy in all matters pertaining to the group.

Bush had the name, the record, and the connections to immediately follow his father into Wall Street affluence but, wanting to make his own name, he instead headed to the heat-drenched fields of west Texas to work for an oil field supply company called Dresser Industries. Bush believed that the economy would boom now that the war had ended, and since every business needed fuel, he figured that was the place to make his fortune. Bush swept warehouse floors and painted and repaired machine parts. He worked so hard that coworkers joked his middle initials, H. W.,

stood for "Hard Work." His boss, Bill Nelson, would compile a list of things for Bush to do the next day, only to find that the young associate had already completed most items on the list.

After a brief stint in California, as a traveling salesman for the company, Bush returned to Midland, Texas, where he started the first in a succession of firms that specialized in locating and producing oil. Through the 1950s he guided his businesses to success and became one of the first millionaires in the area. In 1958, to be closer to his offshore oil drilling operation, Bush moved the family to Houston.

He and Barbara experienced joy and sadness on the personal front. Their son George W. was born in 1947, followed by three more sons and two daughters by 1959. Unfortunately, daughter Robin was

---

*In the 1950s Bush became involved in offshore oil drilling in Houston, Texas.*

diagnosed with leukemia at the age of three. The Bushes flew their daughter to one of the finest cancer research facilities in the nation in hopes of finding a cure, but none existed.

The arduous eight-month illness deeply affected Bush. Each morning at 6:30 he stopped in the local church to say a few prayers. Barbara recalled that her husband could not bear to see his little girl suffer. "Poor George had the most dreadful time and could hardly stand to see her get a blood transfusion. He would say that he had to go to the men's room. We used to laugh and wonder if Robin thought he had the weakest bladder in the world. Not true. He just had the most tender heart."[7] Robin died in 1953, just before her fourth birthday. While his daughter's illness progressed, Bush could not ignore his business and professional pursuits.

Now that Bush had established himself as a successful businessman, he entered the political realm. Few candidates had what he offered—youth, good looks, solid family ties, a heroic war record—but he ran for senator as a Republican in Texas, a heavily Democratic state. In 1964 he took a leave of absence from his business to campaign for the Republican nomination for U.S. senator. After defeating three candidates, he faced the Democratic incumbent, Ralph Yarborough, a staunch ally of the current president, Texan Lyndon B. Johnson. Bush lost the general election, but his 43.5 percent showing was the best any Republican had done in Texas history.

Two years later Bush won his first race when he defeated Frank Briscoe to gain a seat in the House of Representatives from Texas's Seventh District. In achieving victory, Bush employed a personal touch to campaigning by going door-to-door to meet as many voters as possible. With rolled-up sleeves and his coat slung over his shoulder, he handed out political leaflets and stood in front of businesses to shake hands.

The tactics worked admirably. The *Wall Street Journal* placed Bush among "the large number of new and appealing Republican personalities across the nation,"[8] and Bush swept into office by earning 57.6 percent of the vote in a heavily Democratic district. To avoid any possible charges that he would act politically to help his commercial enterprise, Bush sold his business interests for over $1 million shortly before moving to Washington, D.C.

Bush gained a reputation as a conservative who supported the Vietnam War and opposed a large budget, but he also was respected as a man who voted his conscience. He advocated giving the right to vote to eighteen-year-olds and abolishing the draft, and he astonished Texas political observers by voting for the Fair Housing Act of 1968, a measure that many Texans hated since it banned discrimination in the selling of homes.

He also believed in the right to protest, which many other conservative politicians detested. He argued that Americans had the duty to air their opinions and had the

*As a U.S. representative in the 1960s, Bush supported Americans' right to protest the war in Vietnam.*

right to protest, especially young Americans who were subject to be drafted and sent to Vietnam. He ordered his staff to interrupt him whenever a group of young people arrived to talk with him so he could come out and give them a chance to be heard.

He was popular enough to win reelection in 1968, but not so two years later. With the Republicans in charge of the White House under Richard Nixon, Bush felt that the time was proper for him to try again for the Senate. Despite assistance from the president, Bush lost the election to Lloyd Bentsen, an influential Texan who lined up formidable support among the Democrats.

Since he had to give up his House seat to campaign for the Senate, Bush joined the ranks of the unemployed when he lost to Bentsen. Nixon rectified the situation by naming him the U.S. ambassador to the United Nations in December 1970. In 1972 Nixon asked him to become the chairman of the Republican Party, a powerful post since the chairman helps decide who receives Republican funds and other support. This position pushed Bush to the upper levels of his party. He worked hard to improve the chances of fellow Republicans in House and Senate races, but his efforts were hampered by Nixon's growing involvement in the Watergate scandal, in which burglars broke into the Democratic headquarters at the Watergate Hotel. At first Bush supported the president, but when tapes appeared that proved Nixon had obstructed an FBI investigation into the burglary, Bush wrote a letter to Nixon requesting he resign.

Nixon's successor, Gerald Ford, appointed Bush as chief of the liaison office in the People's Republic of China in October 1974, a post similar to that of ambassador. Since the United States and China did not then have full diplomatic relations, this post handled American matters in China until a complete embassy with ambassador could be negotiated and put in place.

Following that assignment, Bush was named head of the Central Intelligence Agency (CIA) in January 1976. The president hoped that Bush could bring his diplomatic and executive skills, honed in the oil fields of Texas and the liaison office in China, to the troubled CIA, which was then awash in controversy. Many instances of previous abuses by CIA operatives in gathering information had surfaced shortly before Bush took over. CIA operatives had been accused of being involved in assassination attempts against Cuban dictator Fidel Castro and conducting experiments with mind-controlling drugs. He took swift action to remedy the situation.

Bush instituted measures that gave him more control over CIA operations and allowed a freer discussion of CIA matters with Congress. In less than one year, Bush made fifty-one visits to Capitol Hill to brief representatives on CIA activities. This unheard of number of appearances not only kept politicians informed but made them more likely to support the CIA rather than attack it. Bush's insistence on a code of ethics, which emphasized honesty and the avoidance of secret experiments, helped prevent further controversies and restored morale to a battered agency. One top CIA operative claimed that Bush restored dignity to the organization.

## Presidential Politics

By 1977 Bush felt confident enough to mount his first campaign for the presidency. He believed that his years in various governmental capacities, combined with his success as a businessman, provided him with the tools needed to be the nation's leader. Besides, he loved politics and was confident he could fashion a program that appealed to voters.

He established a Bush-for-president campaign organization in 1977, and in May 1979 he formally announced his intention to seek the Republican nomination in 1980. After an impressive victory in Iowa over Ronald Reagan in the year's first primary election, Bush's campaign sputtered. When Reagan won in Bush's home state of Texas, Bush withdrew from the race.

To unite the party, Reagan offered the vice presidential slot to George Bush. The two formed an attractive team that combined Reagan's charisma with the younger Bush's foreign policy experience and less conservative bent. The move worked, as the pair collected enough support to take a

November 1980 win over the incumbent president, Jimmy Carter.

As vice president, Bush held no real power. He gave hundreds of speeches around the nation and entertained important dignitaries from foreign lands, but his primary duty was to be prepared to assume office in case something happened to the president. As such, he attended daily national security briefings with Reagan and ate lunch with the president once each week, where Reagan kept him informed of important matters.

Bush did not recede into the background as many vice presidents do. Colin

Powell recalled one briefing about drugs where Bush "argued with the President directly in front of the rest of us."[9] While Bush failed to convince Reagan, Powell was impressed by the vice president's willingness to advocate his own views.

On March 30, 1981, tragedy occurred when an assassin attempted to kill President Reagan. As the stricken leader recovered in a hospital that night, Bush earned high marks for his calm handling

*Bush (right) served two terms as vice president of the United States under President Ronald Reagan (left).*

of the crisis and for easing the public's fears that the government had been immobilized by the incident.

Bush served as vice president for eight years. In 1988 he handily won the Republican nomination for president, then selected Indiana senator Dan Quayle as his running mate. The controversial choice raised many eyebrows, since the staunchly conservative senator lacked experience in foreign policy, was a poor public speaker, had not served in Vietnam, and had gained lackluster grades through college.

The divisive campaign featured a statement that returned to haunt Bush later. To reinforce his pledge to avoid raising taxes, Bush produced his famous words, "Read my lips—no new taxes." The catchy phrase helped elect him to office, but when taxes had to be imposed during his presidency, he lost credibility in some circles. Bush won the general election in November over Michael Dukakis and was sworn in as president on January 20, 1989. He became the first vice president elected directly to the presidency since Martin Van Buren in 1837.

Foreign affairs dominated the Bush presidency. As the Soviet Union collapsed and removed the threat of communism, Bush extended a hand to the Soviet leader, Mikhail Gorbachev. He negotiated arms reduction treaties with the country and offered financial assistance and words of encouragement to the leader, who boldly implemented reforms into Russian society.

When a rebel group tried to oust Filipino leader Corazon Aquino in late 1989, she requested help from the Bush administration. Bush ordered jet aircraft to fly low over the presidential place in the Philippines as a sign of support, and the rebel forces melted into the jungles.

His first big crisis came in Panama, where the government of Manuel Noriega had trampled on the democratic rights of his people, threatened American citizens residing in the region, and participated in drug trafficking. After a series of Panamanian abuses against American citizens, in December 1989 Bush ordered twenty-six thousand soldiers into the nation to capture Noriega and safeguard American interests. A speedy operation succeeded in capturing Noriega, who was flown to Florida to stand trial for his illegal drug activities.

Following the invasion, President Bush and his wife visited injured soldiers in a hospital. Barbara Bush later wrote, "The most moving moment came when a paraplegic said as we were leaving, 'Sir, I wanted to give you this flag. It represents my buddies in Panama. We're proud of you and back you.' That flag was on George's desk in the Oval Office until we left on January 20, 1993, and is now on his desk in Houston."[10]

## The Gulf War

A president has numerous areas to handle during a war. While the generals and admirals implement strategy, the president explains war aims to the nation, ensures cooperating nations remain satisfied, and garners support for the endeavor. Bush's

## Troops Move into Panama

One of the closest observers to what transpired in the White House during the Bush presidency was, of course, his wife Barbara. She confided her thoughts about her husband's actions in Panama to her diary, which is included in her 1994 autobiography, *Barbara Bush: A Memoir*.

On Wednesday morning George sent troops into Panama for many valid reasons. #1. They had elections several months ago and Noriega was beaten three to one and yet he overturned the people's vote and took power. #2. He declared war on the USA and then a Marine officer was murdered. #3. His troops harassed a Naval officer, beat him and his wife and sexually threatened his wife. #4. We have thousands of American citizens in Panama. #5. They have violated our treaty.

military background, combined with Vietnam experience, enabled him to better understand the needs of the military and of the nation, and better explain how the two coincided.

When Iraq's Saddam Hussein sent his army into Kuwait, Bush and the United Nations warned that military steps loomed unless he withdrew. That region, which held a great portion of the world's oil supply, was too important to let any dictator control its valuable resources, so Bush realized that the possibility for war was great.

He first had to prepare the United States for any military action. He knew that he might soon be asking fathers and mothers to allow him to send their sons and daughters into the battlefield, so he had to gain their complete backing. He told his staff near Christmas 1990, "I have resolved all moral questions in my mind. This is black and white, good versus evil."[11] But he also had to convince fellow politicians, the world, and the nation.

Bush mounted a clever campaign to line up support. He first gained the approval of the United Nations, then approached Congress about adopting a resolution approving the use of force. Senators and members of the House of Representatives had little choice but to adopt the resolution, for the nation would appear unreliable should the president achieve support from the world and fail to gain it at home.

Bush attempted to explain the goals of the military action in speeches around the nation. He hoped that every parent knew that the United States had sent its military to halt Iraqi aggression, but he had doubts as war drew near. On Christmas Eve 1990 he confided to his diary, "It's Christmas Eve, and you think of the families and loved ones apart. I read ten or fifteen letters, all of them saying, 'Take care of my kid.' Then I sit here knowing that if there is no movement on Saddam's part, we have to go to war."[12]

Shortly before the opening of hostilities, Bush sent a final appeal to Saddam Hussein. Delivered in Geneva, Switzerland, to the Iraqi foreign minister Tariq Aziz by American secretary of state James Baker, the letter stated that the two nations stood at the brink of war because of Hussein's aggression. "I am writing you now, directly, because what is at stake demands that no opportunity be lost to avoid what would be a certain calamity for the people of Iraq."[13]

Bush knew that his letter had little chance of swaying Hussein, but it allowed him to claim to the American people that he had done everything to avoid war. He understood that only by being reassured that the government had tried to avert war, would the public accept it once it began.

In his speech to the nation two hours after the air attack commenced in January, Bush reiterated the reasons for using force. He reminded the nation that in the 1930s European countries had done nothing to restrain Adolf Hitler, and World War II resulted. He said that he would not allow Saddam Hussein to do the same. Bush then spoke about creating "a new world order, a world where the rule of law, not the law of the jungle, governs the conduct of nations."[14]

## One Step Ahead

Domino's Pizza attempts to outperform its competitors, but they may never have enjoyed a more unusual advantage than the one they had on the night of January 16, 1991. When the Washington, D.C. Domino's stores received record orders for pizzas from the White House and the Pentagon, executives concluded it meant that workers had to remain at the two locations all night. They decided that war would commence the next day and spread the news to its stores throughout the nation.

To avoid the errors of Vietnam, he decided not to interfere with his military commanders once the war started. He wrote in his diary after meeting with Gen. Norman Schwarzkopf, "I am convinced more than ever that we can knock Saddam Hussein out early, I'm worried that the American people might think this will be another Vietnam and it isn't and it won't be."[15] He declared in his speech to the nation shortly after the war started that the troops would be given whatever they needed to do the job quickly and that the casualties would be held to a minimum.

Bush coordinated the opening moves to the war, then stepped aside to allow the military to carry out its tasks. When the fighting subsided, he reentered the picture to decide when the war should end. On February 27 Bush met with the chairman of the Joint Chiefs of Staff, Colin Powell, and learned that the ground assault begun only three days earlier had gone much better than expected. American marines had pushed on toward Kuwait City ahead of schedule, and American army units were then swinging behind the Iraqi forces against light opposition in their attempt to surround Hussein's army. Powell mentioned that the Iraqi army was in disarray and that the coalition forces should wrap things up the next day. Bush asked, "If that's the case, why not end it today?"[16] If the war could be ended earlier, lives could be saved.

Bush believed that the war's objectives—forcing Iraq out of Kuwait and de-

*Bush achieved his aim of incapacitating Hussein's military. Here, an Iraqi tank burns after an attack during Operation Desert Storm in 1991.*

stroying Hussein's capabilities to make war—had been accomplished and thus there was no further need to keep American troops on the battlefield. Some urged him to allow the American forces to continue fighting all the way to the Iraqi capital, Baghdad, but he worried that would bring about a lengthy American occupation of Iraq and divide the nation. He was willing to accept the criticism that would inevitably follow should Hussein, the man he depicted as the devil incarnate, remain in power. When Hussein subsequently held onto the reins of office, Bush had to deal with heavy public criticism.

Besides, Bush was concerned that televised images of burning destroyed Iraqi

## Powell Assesses Bush

George Bush achieved much in his four years in the White House, even though his tenure was tainted by criticism of how he ended the Gulf War. Colin Powell worked as closely with George Bush as any military man, and he came away with great admiration for the man. He explains his feelings in his autobiography, *My American Journey.*

> The George Bush I served was a patrician born to privilege in New England, yet made it on his own in Texas oil fields; a well-bred gentleman who was also full of mischief and fun to be around. He was fair-minded in his judgment and treatment of individuals, yet seemed unmindful of the racial polarization being caused by the far right wing of his party. He had given America proud victories in Panama and the Persian Gulf, presided over the end of the Cold War, and left a world safer from nuclear catastrophe.

equipment and forces gave the impression that American forces were inflicting needless carnage on their foe. Bush and Powell decided to end the war at midnight, making it the "Hundred Hour War."

Not every leader agreed with Bush's decision to end the war when he did. Margaret Thatcher, British prime minister during part of the conflict, was stunned that Bush would stop before removing Hussein from power. She claimed that much of the Iraqi army remained in the field and that Hussein would one day cause more problems. "Those people should have been seen to have been defeated. They should have

surrendered their equipment and their armed forces." Thatcher added that "The people of Iraq never saw this dictator humiliated and beaten."[17]

Many benefits accrued to Bush after the war. He received high marks for allowing the military to decide what it needed, then giving them room to accomplish their goals. The victory ended the specter of Vietnam that haunted the nation and the military. *Time* magazine began one article with the words, "Hello, Kuwait. Goodbye, Vietnam," then concluded, "When the U.S.-led forces raced across Kuwait and Iraq last week, however, they may have defeated not just the Iraqi army but also the more virulent of the ghosts from the Vietnam era: self-doubt, fear of power, divisiveness, a fundamental uncertainty about America's purpose in the world."[18]

Bush helped orchestrate a victory by handling the public relations aspect while giving the military free rein. As military analyst Rick Atkinson concluded, "It's hard to see that his presidency will be remembered for anything greater than his performance during the war."[19]

### After the War

George Bush remained in office for another year and a half after the Gulf War ended. He rode a high wave of popularity for a time, but his decision to allow Hussein to remain in office eroded support. Other difficulties with a stagnant economy, high budget deficit, and crime and violence in the nation's large cities dropped his approval rating.

In November 1992 Bush lost the presidential election to Arkansas governor Bill Clinton. George Bush remained active. He and his wife moved to Houston, where they raised money for charity, wrote popular memoirs, and planned and opened a presidential library at Texas A&M.

As always, Bush provided an example to his children. His oldest son George W. Bush later wrote,

Dad jumped out of an airplane [the president followed through on one of his longtime dreams of parachuting from an aircraft]; Mom (and most of the rest of us) thought he was crazy, but he savored the moment like a big, giddy kid. Life was good. And so was their example. We saw, firsthand, that you could enter the arena, give it your best, and leave with your integrity intact. We saw that there is life after losing. [20]

# Chapter 2

# Saddam Hussein: Mideast Revolutionary

One of the most enigmatic individuals to play a crucial role in the Persian Gulf War was Iraqi president Saddam Hussein. On the one hand intelligent, loving toward his family, and conscious that his people deserve the benefits of an expanding economy, Hussein could also resort to extreme ruthlessness in crushing opponents, inside and outside of his country.

## Early Life

Saddam Hussein al-Tikriti, the second of two sons, was born on April 28, 1937, in a mud house outside of Tikrit, a small Iraqi town north of Baghdad. Besides producing textile and leather goods, Tikrit earned a reputation as being the birthplace of the esteemed twelfth-century sultan, Saladin.

Saddam's early years produced little joy. Because his mother was unmarried when she became pregnant with Saddam, many village residents considered him an outcast and most of his schoolmates viciously

taunted him. The unpopular boy often carried an iron bar with him to fend off attackers. The windowless run-down hut with dirt walls in which he lived had no electricity or water. His father died shortly after Saddam's birth, and his mother married Ibrahim Hassan, a man who treated Saddam like an animal. He told Saddam he was no better than a dog, and forced Saddam to steal chickens and sheep so Ibrahim could make money by reselling the pilfered items. Eventually, the family grew to five children with the birth of three half-brothers, Barzan, Sawabi, and Watban Ibrahim [in addition to older brother Hassan].

One day his cousin, Adnan Khairallah, visited from Tikrit and showed Saddam how to write a few letters from the alphabet. The intrigued youngster begged his mother and stepfather for permission to go to school, but they replied that he was needed to take care of the animals.

Set on acquiring an education, one night the ten-year-old Saddam gathered his sparse belongings, sneaked away from the hut, and walked for two hours to the village of Al Fatha. Relatives then escorted him to Tikrit, where he stayed with his uncle, Hajj Khairallah, and attended school.

His uncle exerted profound influence on the young Saddam by taking him under his wing and introducing him to the family business. Unfortunately Khairallah, a former army officer who lost his commission and spent time in prison for his rebellious activities, ran a profitable criminal business that controlled local government and commercial concerns. Saddam enthusiastically joined his uncle's organization, and before his sixteenth birthday he had murdered his first victim—a distant relative who had angered Khairallah.

A few years later Saddam and his uncle participated in the murder of a local civil servant. Saddam was arrested by government officials, but he was released when they could not collect sufficient evidence to prove his part. These events, however, brought Saddam's name to the notice of the Baath Socialist Party, an organization dedicated to achieving Arab rule for Iraq.

Like many males in Iraq, including Uncle Khairallah, Saddam developed a hatred for Great Britain. During World War

I thirty years earlier, many Arab leaders established a friendly relationship with the British because the country controlling Iraq, the Ottoman Empire, had aligned with Britain's enemy, Germany. As soon as

*Saddam Hussein (pictured) left an unhappy home at age ten to live with his uncle Khairallah.*

the war ended, however, Britain and France occupied many of the same lands that the Ottoman Empire had controlled. In Iraqi eyes, one plundering country had simply replaced another. Tikrit especially suffered because the British brought into Iraq their own leather and textile goods, a step that devastated Tikrit's economy. As a result, the town became a hotbed of political unrest and anti-British sentiment.

Conditions deteriorated during World War II. Many Iraqis favored the Germans, and in 1941 a group revolted against the British-supported Iraqi monarchy. Because of their role in the uprising, several of Saddam's relatives were executed, and his uncle, Hajj Khairallah, was forced out of the military.

## Involvement in Politics

In the fall of 1955 Saddam Hussein, supported by Khairallah's money, traveled to Baghdad to study at the al-Karkh secondary school. While there he joined student activist groups and became more

### Family Name

According to Arab custom, each portion of a name signifies something. For instance, the name Saddam Hussein al-Tikriti is broken down in the following manner:

—"Saddam" means "He who faces the aggressor"

—"Hussein" was his father's first name

—"al-Tikriti" means "from Tikrit"

deeply involved with the Arab Baath Socialist Party. The next year Hussein participated in an abortive attempt to oust the current Iraqi ruler, King Faisal II, but evaded a furious search for conspirators by government troops.

Another political group succeeded in changing the government before the Baath Party. An opponent of the Baath Party, the pro-Communist military leader, Abdul Karim Kassem, organized a military takeover in 1958 and executed King Faisal. He declared Iraq a republic and established ties with the Soviet Union, then instituted a ruthless campaign to hunt down political rivals, especially members of the Baath party. When one of Kassem's government officials was assassinated in 1959 in Tikrit, Hussein was among those opponents who were arrested, tortured, and confined in prison. A few months later, after repeated beatings and punishments by electric shock, officials dropped the charges and set Hussein free.

It may have been a mistake on their part. In October 1959, Baath Party officials selected Hussein and nine other members to carry out the assassination of Kassem. The plan called for most of the men to rush Kassem's car as it drove by on the way to his office and pepper the vehicle with bullets. Hussein received orders to stay back and cover the others.

In late October Hussein and the others spread out along Baghdad's main thoroughfare, Rashid Street, and waited for Kassem's car. Upon spotting it, Hussein's cohorts ran

*In 1959 Hussein participated in an attempt to assassinate the pro-Communist leader of Iraq, Abdul Karim Kassem (pictured).*

up and started firing. In the excitement, Hussein forgot his assignment and joined the others. Though the ten men riddled the vehicle with bullets and killed two body-guards, Kassem escaped unharmed. Hussein

limped away with a wound to his leg.

The next morning he and a friend removed the bullet with scissors and a razor blade. Hussein then attended school as if it were a normal day to avoid arousing suspicion, but when he learned later in the day that his companions had been arrested, Hussein hurried home, packed a few belongings, and hustled out of town. Fifteen minutes later, Kassem's police burst through the door looking for Hussein.

After hiding in a relative's house outside Baghdad, Hussein donned long robes and, disguised as a desert Bedouin, started for Tikrit on horseback. For three days he successfully evaded police and finally arrived at a village across a river from Tikrit. Hussein waited until nightfall, then swam across the frigid river with his clothes tied in a bundle and a knife glistening between his teeth. He later explained that he almost succumbed in the middle of the river because of the swift current and cold temperatures, but he finally reached the other side, crawled out, put on his wet clothes, and convinced a local family to hide him for the night. The following day he arrived at his mother's house, rested awhile, then rode a donkey across the desert to Syria.

In the spring of 1960 he traveled to Egypt, where Egyptian president Gamal Abdel Nasser guaranteed his safety. Hussein loved his tenure in the friendly nation, where he observed Nasser's measures to forge a potent Arab community in his nation and elsewhere in the Mideast. Hussein was captivated by the thought of removing Western control from his homeland, uniting Arab people in the region, and restoring the dignity once held by Saladin, something Nasser referred to with his slogan, "Humiliation is over."

After graduating from Egypt's al-Qasr al-Aini secondary school in 1961, Hussein attended the University of Cairo's law school the next year. Before he completed his studies, the Baath Party wrested control of the Iraqi government from Kassem and executed the leader. Hussein decided that it was time to return home.

## Back in Iraq

Hussein arrived in Iraq in February 1963, and shortly afterward married his first cousin, Sajida Talfah, a teacher. The two subsequently raised sons Udai and Qusai, and daughters Raghad, Rina, and Hala.

Baath officials gave Hussein the task of organizing and spreading the party's policies to the uneducated masses in Iraq, and he did so well that he came to the attention of party cofounder Michel Aflaq. The leader praised Hussein's calmness and clear sense of purpose. Unfortunately, the Baath Party did not long remain in power in unstable Iraq, where rival factions frequently ousted one another from office. Before the year ended another group forced the Baath Party out, but Aflaq and other Baath leaders vowed to return. They placed Hussein in charge of its military arm and ordered him to plan a takeover for 1964. On September 4, 1964, one day before the scheduled revolt, police uncovered the plot and, following a gunfight, arrested the conspirators. Hussein was among those apprehended and sent to prison for two years.

Even while incarcerated Hussein kept his name in front of his followers. He studied law to improve his grasp of international affairs and was even elected deputy secretary of the Baath Party's regional leadership. When he learned that his party planned another coup, Hussein slipped away from his guards, fled into hiding, and helped orchestrate the coming revolt.

A July 1968 coup returned the Baath Party to power. Hussein and Maj. Gen. Ahmed Hassan al-Bakr were chosen to rule together. Hussein served as the acting deputy chairman of the Revolutionary Command Council until 1969, when he was named deputy chairman. While al-Bakr held the more important title of president, Hussein actually ran the government for his ailing comrade.

## Hussein in Control

Hussein's dual personality was exemplified in the way he ruled his nation. While he and al-Bakr imposed a harsh regime on their country, highlighted by executions and torture of political opponents, Hussein also supported programs designed to improve life for the masses and forge a strong Arab community. For example, Hussein believed that everyone in his nation should learn to read and write.

Hussein exemplified ruthlessness in pursuit of control. He supposedly studied law during these years, but according to a news report in the *London Observer*, he received the law degree by simply turning up in the examination hall with a pistol in his belt and accompanied by four armed bodyguards. The examiners overseeing the test passed Hussein without question. To consolidate power, he arranged to be promoted to full general in 1976, then had it made retroactive to 1973 so he would have seniority over other Iraqi generals.

The Iraqi criminal code developed by Hussein listed twenty offenses punishable by death, including execution for anyone who publicly insulted Saddam Hussein. Hussein employed five separate security forces to ensure he controlled every aspect of government and business life and to place fear among those who might think of opposing him.

He often exhibited extreme ruthlessness in eliminating rivals. Among the mass killings orchestrated by Hussein were that of the Iraqi Jews in 1969 and the Shiites in 1970 and 1972. His dictatorial measures produced a string of unsuccessful opposition coups by groups who wanted to re-

*Hussein took control of the foreign-owned Iraq Petroleum Company in 1972 and used the profits to launch programs to modernize Iraq.*

place Hussein with a more moderate leader. Following one failed attempt in June 1973 by Iraqi communists, Hussein ordered tortures and executions on such a large scale that Amnesty International, a worldwide organization that promotes fair treatment, classed Iraq as one of the worst violators of human rights.

On the other hand, Hussein pushed for an improved economy and freedom from foreign interests. In 1972 he nationalized (took over) the Iraq Petroleum Company, a foreign-controlled firm that produced 10 percent of the Mideast oil,

*Hussein (shown here visiting children) is lauded by some Iraqis for his efforts to create a modern, prosperous nation.*

so Iraq could benefit. Hussein invested the enormous profits from this and other oil ventures into modernization programs. Baghdad and other cities bustled with projects constructing new hospitals, homes, water purification plants, electrical power plants, and new highways. To ensure his people would be prepared for the technological world of the future, in 1978 he commenced a mandatory literacy campaign.

Journalist Michael Kelly visited Iraq and interviewed a number of Iraqi citizens. He found that while some people feared Hussein, others enjoyed the new prosperity that he seemed to have created. Kelly quoted one man as saying of Baghdad,

Look around. When I was a child, this city was like a village. A big village, that is all. Your hotel—it did not exist. The roads—they did not exist. Saddam built it all. He built many roads, many schools, many hospitals. Everything, Saddam built. In the past, people did not have shoes. Now they have cars.[21]

Hussein's foreign policy produced few surprises. Like most Arab leaders, he refused to negotiate with Israel and hoped to see the day when the country was wiped off the earth. Carved from land that had been held by Arab nations for more than a thousand years, the Jewish state in the midst of Arab nations produced animosity and vows of vengeance. Israel contended it had a right to the land, but Arab states countered that Israel had no claims for territory that had been in Arab control for so long. In October 1973 Hussein dispatched eighteen thousand soldiers to fight with Syria in its war with Israel, and relations with the United States fluctuated from bad to worse depending on the amount of American aid to the Jewish state.

Hussein established close ties with the Soviet Union by signing a fifteen-year treaty of friendship. A steady stream of arms poured into Iraq from the communist nation in return for a communist presence in the party's leadership. This alliance entered shaky ground in 1978 when Hussein ordered the execution of twenty-one communists suspected of participating in a planned coup.

## Assassination Attempt

Other events helped Hussein further consolidate his control of the Iraqi government. Due to illness, Hassan al-Bakr stepped down in July 1979. Though Hussein had been in charge all along, he now added al-Bakr's titles to his long list. He appointed family members and close friends to serve as his chief advisers, and while this gave Hussein a feeling of security, it surrounded him with

people who would not dare argue with Hussein or tell him he was wrong.

U.S. ambassador to Iraq, David G. Newton, said that Hussein was "a tough, ruthless, hard-nosed, intelligent and sometimes brutal leader who is used to getting his own way."[22] Stories circulated that Hussein enjoyed the gruesome practice of watching videotapes of executions, and political opponents spoke with caution, if at all. Soon after becoming president, Hussein learned of a plot to overthrow his government, the latest in a lengthy line of assassination attempts made against the dictator. He decided that the time had arrived to cleanse the Baath party of anyone he deemed disloyal. A wave of arrests gathered government ministers, political leaders, and party workers and placed them in front of firing squads.

A former Iraqi cabinet member recalled the August 1979 incident. "The party officials were handed machine guns. One by one the guards brought in the accused, their mouths taped shut, and their hands bound. Hussein asked everyone to start shooting. At least 21 were killed, and every victim received at least 500 bullets in his body."[23] Amnesty International and other human rights groups castigated the Iraqi leader for the massacre.

Hussein tried to win the support of his countrymen. Television cameras from the state-controlled station pictured him visiting children in school or workers in the fields, and he installed a special telephone line so that private citizens could call him with their problems. Propaganda broadcasts and articles compared Hussein to revered Arab leaders such as Nebuchadrezzar, the famed Babylonian king who destroyed Jerusalem in 587 B.C., or Saladin, who successfully battled Christian crusaders.

Benefiting from immense oil profits, Hussein added more social programs. Higher education and medical care became available to anyone, and within three years illiteracy had been practically eradicated. He extended the vote to women in time for the 1980 parliamentary elections, and he encouraged females to run for political office. Hussein's wife, a schoolteacher, appeared in public to promote increased contributions to society by females.

## War with Iran

Hussein's domestic concerns diminished in importance in the early 1980s when trouble with Iran brewed. In February 1979 the fundamentalist religious leader Ayatollah Khomeini returned from exile after Iran's leader, the shah of Iran, had been overthrown in a revolution. Hoping to spread his brand of Islam throughout the Middle East, Khomeini called on fundamentalists in Iraq to rebel against Hussein and join Iran in an Islamic revolution. He claimed that Kuwait, Bahrain, and southern Iraq belonged to Iran and that he would support the Kurdish rebels of northern Iraq in their struggle against their arch rival, Hussein.

On April 1, 1980, Hussein's deputy prime minister, Tariq Aziz, was delivering a speech to college students when someone tossed a bomb toward him. Aziz fell to the ground and avoided injury, but many students in the audience were wounded and killed. When Iraq's pro-Khomeini party, Al Dawa-Al Islam, took credit for the assault, Hussein vowed revenge. The party's second most important leader, Mohammed Bakr Sadr, was quickly arrested.

Another bomb exploded four days later, this time in the midst of the funeral procession organized for the college students killed in the first incident. Saddam executed Bakr Sadr and members of his family, then expelled from the country thirty-thousand Iraqis of Iranian descent. At the same time he offered to assist Iranian dissidents who hoped to overthrow Khomeini.

Events heated to an ominous point. Iranian forces moved closer to the Iraqi border and shelled a few positions. Hussein worried that conditions inside Iran would force either the United States or the Soviet Union to intervene as a way of protecting their oil interests, a move that would prevent Hussein from establishing his own sphere of influence in the region. To avoid this, on September 2, 1980, he launched an air and land attack on Iran. Within one week his armies seized a forty-five-mile-wide stretch of land inside Iran.

Backed by U.S. and Israeli support in the form of weapons, the Iranian army surprisingly fought the Iraqi army to a standstill. For the next eighteen months Iran and Iraq battled back and forth across Iranian soil. In the spring of 1982 Iran, with careless disregard for loss of life, sent wave after wave of poorly armed soldiers to attack Iraqi positions. In spite of the enormous slaughter they absorbed, Iran forced Iraq back to the original borders between the two nations.

In July Iran entered Iraqi territory. For the next two years the advantage remained with Khomeini's forces, as his troops grabbed more land from Hussein. Due to the war's exorbitant cost, and because Syria had shut down the Iraqi oil pipeline running through their land, Hussein had to institute severe cost-cutting measures. His social programs withered, and food became scarcer.

*Iranian forces storm into Iraq during the Iran-Iraq War, a bloody conflict lasting from 1980 to 1988.*

He also resorted to more terrifying measures to defeat Iran. After Iranian troops cut the highway from Baghdad to Basra in eastern Iraq, Hussein used chemical weapons, which again brought condemnation throughout the world. Iranian forces seized the Fao Peninsula in southeast Iraq, then moved their artillery within range of the crucial town of Basra, near Kuwait. Iraqi citizens, already suffering from drastic cuts imposed by the war, fled Basra.

As Iran moved closer to major sections of Iraq, Hussein's soldiers stiffened. After three months of hard fighting they pushed their enemy back from Basra and regained possession of the Fao Peninsula. When his troops maintained the drive and kept Iranian units reeling backward, Hussein believed that he had won the war.

Khomeini suffered horrific losses in the campaign against Hussein. At least five hundred thousand Iranians, many of them under eighteen years old, perished in the eight-year struggle. Seeing his forces in retreat, Khomeini agreed to a cease-fire on July 18, 1988. Hussein once more turned to the needs of his shattered country.

## Strife with the United States

"The Iraqi army had made me uncomfortable ever since Iraq and Iran ended their bloody eight-year war in 1988, while I was National Security Advisor," wrote Colin Powell. "Once Saddam, with an army over one million men strong, no longer had Iran

## Powell Expresses Surprise

Colin Powell could not believe that Hussein so recklessly marched toward war with the United States. He worried what the Iraqi dictator might do with his huge army, but once the United Nations took action against Iraq, Powell thought Hussein would retreat. He wrote of his astonishment in his autobiography, *My American Journey*.

> I was amazed, given the forces and power now arrayed against Saddam Hussein, unmatched since D-Day, that he still had not blinked, still he kept barreling down the highway to disaster. He had to know that he would lose, but as long as he could survive in power, he was apparently willing to pay the price for his Kuwait adventure in dead Iraqis.

to worry about, I feared he would look for mischief somewhere else."[24]

Powell could not have been more farsighted. Relations between Hussein and the United States, never good because of the American commitment to Israel, deteriorated during the Iran–Iraq war. In November 1986 Hussein learned that in exchange for the release of American hostages taken captive in Lebanon, the United States was selling missiles to Iran, which Khomeini then used to seize the Fao Peninsula.

The United States threatened reprisals when Iraqi missiles hit an American ship in the Persian Gulf on May 17, 1987, killing thirty-seven Americans. Hussein explained that it had been a case of mistaken identity, which the United States accepted, but the two nations viewed each other with considerable suspicion.

Conditions worsened over Iraq's clash with Kuwait. Hussein hoped to rebuild his nation following the ruinous war with Iran, but Kuwait, a nation on its southeast border, posed problems. While Hussein's attention was turned toward Iran, Kuwaiti forces advanced into what Hussein considered a part of Iraq. A Kuwaiti spokesman then announced that the nation would produce an unlimited amount of oil, which had the effect of dropping oil prices from eighteen dollars a barrel to eleven dollars. Since Iraq heavily depended on oil profits, this reduction by one-third devastated Hussein's attempt to bring prosperity to his land.

The final insult, as far as Hussein was concerned, happened when Kuwait demanded he repay the money Iraq had borrowed from Kuwait during the Iran–Iraq war. Hussein believed that he fought against Khomeini for every Arab nation and that he had extinguished any debt with the blood of his soldiers.

Hussein threatened that if Kuwait did not pull out of the occupied lands and forget about the debt, he would take military action. When no satisfactory reply followed, Hussein moved troops to the Kuwaiti border on July 18, 1990. Walter P. Lang, a senior intelligence analyst for the United States, believed that Hussein intended to strike into Kuwait. "I do not believe he is bluffing. I have looked at his personality profile. He doesn't know how to bluff. It is not in his past pattern of behavior."[25]

On August 2, 1990, more than one hundred thousand Iraqi soldiers poured across the border into Kuwait. They encountered minor opposition, and by noon they had seized Kuwait City and forced the nation's ruler, Jaber Al-Ahmed Al-Sabah, to flee for safety to the U.S. embassy.

American president George Bush worried that Hussein intended to gain control of the Mideast oil market. Since the United States so heavily relied on this source of fuel, Bush vowed he would not allow any single leader to dominate in the area. In an attempt to force Hussein out of Kuwait, Great Britain and the United States convinced the United Nations to announce sanctions against Iraq and forbid trading with that nation. On August 5, President Bush announced that he would never allow Hussein to remain in Kuwait and that he would send American troops overseas to force him out if necessary. The next day Bush started sending the first of thousands of troops across the ocean to protect Saudi Arabia and other portions of the Mideast. He called this Operation Desert Shield.

Hussein did not back down. He shot back to Bush, "You, the President of the United States, have lied to your people. You are going to be defeated. Thousands of Americans whom you have pushed into this dark tunnel will go home shrouded in sad coffins."[26] He then warned his people to prepare for "the mother of all battles."

In a speech to his nation broadcast over radio, Hussein tried to rally his people.

> The despicable Bush and the traitorous Fahd [Saudi Arabia's leader] began their ground offensive this morning. They're attacking our people on the whole breadth of the front. May disgrace cover them. But they'll discover that the great, heroic Iraqi people is superior to them. Fight, oh valorous people of Iraq. Oh, you sons of the mother of all battles, fight to protect your women and children, for you are on the threshold of the highest glory, God's honor. The weapons they have built to fight against us will fall from their hands, and then it will be only a fight between believers [in Allah] and unbelievers. Fight them. Be merciless against them. Have no pity on them.[27]

Events unfolded quickly over the next few months. On August 8 Hussein announced the annexation of Kuwait. The United States responded by forging a coalition of nations around the world, including Arab countries such as Saudi Arabia and Egypt, to oppose Hussein. Bush ordered that the American forces in the region be doubled, and he convinced the United Nations Security Council to pass a resolution authorizing the use of force if Hussein had not pulled out of Kuwait by January 15, 1991.

One final chance at avoiding war occurred when U.S. secretary of state James Baker met with Iraqi foreign minister Tariq Aziz in Geneva, Switzerland, on January 9, 1991. When the meeting failed to produce any agreement, the U.S. Senate voted fifty-two to forty-seven to approve the use of American force against Hussein.

## A Six-Week War

When Hussein failed to pull back from Kuwait, Bush ordered his military into action. In the early morning hours of January 17, successive waves of American aircraft, supported by coalition nations, attacked Baghdad and military targets in Iraq in what was known as Operation Desert Storm. In around-the-clock sorties, Allied fighters and bombers hit command posts, communications centers, congregations of Iraqi soldiers, and supposed locations of Iraqi missiles.

Hussein was apparently taken by surprise at the American offensive. He thought that the United States had been sickened of war following its Vietnam debacle and would have little desire to do anything more than make threats. He told one American diplomat, "Yours is a society which cannot accept 10,000 dead in one battle."[28]

But the American people were ready to engage in warfare, as indicated by an editorial in the *Houston Chronicle* after hostilities opened. The paper proclaimed that Hussein "asked for the war he has gotten. May his God forgive him; we won't."[29] Hussein also grossly underestimated the power that had assembled against him. He had

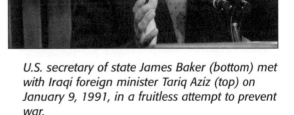

*U.S. secretary of state James Baker (bottom) met with Iraqi foreign minister Tariq Aziz (top) on January 9, 1991, in a fruitless attempt to prevent war.*

little notion of the capabilities of American missiles and fighter-bombers, which relied on laser beams to accurately direct bombs toward their targets.

In retaliation for the American assault, Hussein fired missiles at American targets in Saudi Arabia and toward Israel. If he could prod Israel into military action, Hussein believed that the other Arab nations would cease supporting the United States, and possibly even join Iraq in battling Israel.

Though a few Iraqi missiles inflicted damage—an American barracks was destroyed and Israel suffered losses—Bush succeeded in keeping the coalition forces together. He persuaded Israel to count on the American ability to destroy Iraqi missiles, and he benefited from the Arab world

## Saddam's Threat

Before hostilities started between the United States and Iraq, Saddam Hussein engaged in a war of words with President George Bush in *Time* magazine. Hussein warned in mid-January 1991,

> The Americans will come here to perform acrobatics like Rambo (a popular American fictional movie character who used force to achieve his goals) movies. But they will find here real people to fight them. We are a people who have eight years of experience in war and combat.

watching the events unfold on CNN, the Cable News Network. Leaders in Egypt and elsewhere were repulsed by the sight of one Arab nation hurling missiles into another Arab nation's territory.

The next phase of operations started on February 24 when coalition ground forces, spearheaded by American marines and army units, raced into Kuwait and liberated Kuwait City. Other American units swung to the west behind the Iraqi army in Kuwait and cut off their retreat route to Baghdad. In the next four days coalition forces reduced all pockets of resistance and defeated the Iraqi army. When a cease-fire on January 28 ended the fighting, Iraq had only two intact divisions of soldiers out of the forty-two that existed less than one week earlier. Against Allied losses of 466 killed and 1,287 wounded, Iraq suffered anywhere between 30,000 dead and 100,000 wounded.

## The Aftermath

Hussein's problems, serious before the war, were aggravated by the disastrous Kuwaiti invasion. The economy stood in complete disarray, forcing citizens to scour marketplaces for scraps of food. Power sources lay in ruins, and polluted water threatened to spread illness throughout society. Since President Bush stated that economic sanctions against Iraq would remain until Hussein was out of power, the situation was not likely to improve.

On top of his woes, Hussein had to send the Republican Guard to repress two rebellions. In the south a group of religious dissidents rose up, while to the north the Kurds continued their quest for autonomy. Though the two groups received assistance from the United States, Hussein was able to suppress both factions, often with ghastly brutality. Republican Guard soldiers poured gasoline over one of the rebellious leaders and set him on fire.

As the 1990s wound down to the millennium, Hussein remained in office. He engaged in a lengthy dispute with the United Nations over whether he had dismantled missile sites and followed other dictates of the cease-fire agreement, and his people continued to suffer under the United Nations-imposed trade embargo.

Though his destroyed nation may be far from what Hussein hoped, some military analysts concluded that he may have gained more than he lost in Operation Desert

Storm. He earned the admiration of other Arab nations for standing up to the United States, and if he could remain in power he may have gained a significant base of support to create a more unified Arab world.

Relying on his loyal Republican Guard and an intensive security system that includes hundreds of spies stationed throughout the nation, Hussein has been able to maintain his hold on power. Political opposition exists

*A member of the Kurdish ethnic group in northern Iraq that fought Hussein for independence.*

and unconfirmed reports state that he has been the target of assassination attempts on more than one occasion, but the man who led his country to ruin in the Gulf War remains in office.

That fact must be especially galling to former adversaries. Margaret Thatcher, the prime minister of England during part of the Gulf War, mentioned to a television reporter the irony of the situation. Coalition forces handily defeated the Iraqi army, but "George Bush isn't president anymore. I'm not prime minister. Saddam Hussein is president."[30]

# Chapter 3

# Richard Cheney: Civilian Warrior

The writers of the U.S. Constitution intended that the U.S. government maintain control over the military. Consequently, in every war in U.S. history, government leaders have exerted considerable influence over the top military officials. In the Gulf War, President Bush and his advisers had the final say on all matters. The men allowed great freedom to General Powell and General Schwarzkopf to set the course of war, and only stepped in when necessary. Richard B. Cheney, secretary of defense, provided a superb example of how the government worked with the military toward the common goal of victory.

## Early Life

Richard Bruce Cheney was born on January 30, 1941, in Lincoln, Nebraska, to Richard H. and Marjorie L. Cheney. Government service was no stranger to the Cheney clan, since his father worked as a soil conservationist with the U.S. Department of Agriculture.

When Richard, who preferred to be called Dick, was very young, the family moved to Casper, Wyoming. Dick Cheney attended Natrona County High School, where he enjoyed a carefree life as student, athlete, and outdoorsman. The popular Cheney was named the cocaptain of the football team and was class president in his senior year. After school hours, he loved to hunt and fish in Wyoming's fabulous expanse.

After graduating in 1959, Cheney attended Yale University on a scholarship. The young man was not ready for serious study, however, and dropped out midway through his second year. As he told the *Washington Post*, "I was not well organized in my youth. I didn't like the East, I wasn't a good student. I just wasn't prepared to buckle down."[31]

Cheney returned to Wyoming and took a job erecting and repairing power lines in Wyoming and nearby states. For two years he weighed various alternatives

*During the Persian Gulf War, Secretary of Defense Richard Cheney (left) worked closely with military leaders, including General Colin Powell (right).*

about his future, but the appearance of another individual made Cheney decide that a career as a power lineman was not to be. Cheney fell in love with Lynne Anne Vincent, but he realized that if he were to marry her, he had to offer a more enticing life.

It was clear that Lynne wasn't going to marry a lineman for the county. I had to go make something of myself if I was going to consummate the relationship, and so I went back to school at the University of Wyoming and finished up a B.A. and a master's there and then went to [the University of] Wisconsin and did all the work for my doctorate except the dissertation.[32]

Unlike his tenure at Yale, Cheney compiled an admirable academic record at Wyoming. He even won an essay contest sponsored by New York University's National Center for Education in Politics, and received an internship to the Wyoming state legislature his senior year. Cheney happily accepted the post, even though he had to drive a hundred miles each day from the university to the state capitol in Cheyenne.

Cheney married Lynne Vincent on August 29, 1964. He then completed his B.A. in political science in 1965, and the next year finished his M.A. in the same field. The training provided a sound foundation for his future, as Cheney appeared headed toward government service of some type.

His internships whetted his appetite. He followed his work in Cheyenne with an internship granted by the National Center for Education in Politics. The young man and his bride moved to Madison, Wisconsin, where he worked on the staff of then governor Warren Knowles. In 1968 he accepted a fellowship on the staff of Congressman William Steiger, a Wisconsin Republican with influential ties in Washington, D.C. Steiger so liked the work performed by Cheney that he called the young man "one of the brightest, most perceptive, most sensitive people I've ever had the chance to work with."[33]

Other prominent people agreed with this assessment. Before long, Cheney was working with high government officials in posts few occupy.

## In the White House

Cheney had been fortunate to arrive in Washington, D.C. in 1968, for great changes were occurring. The war in Vietnam soured with the calamitous Tet Offensive, in which the Vietnamese communists mounted widespread attacks on American installations throughout the nation. As a result, the Democrats eventually lost control of both houses in Congress as well as the presidency for the first time in eight years. As a young Republican in the nation's capital, Cheney stared at a golden opportunity to make a name for himself.

He gradually worked his way up in President Richard Nixon's administration. In 1969 Cheney joined the staff of Donald Rumsfeld, the director of the Office of Economic Opportunity. The two immediately forged a close relationship, and Rumsfeld promoted Cheney to special assistant. When in 1970 Rumsfeld was named a presidential counselor, he took Cheney with him as deputy. Barely thirty years old, Cheney occupied an office in the White House.

Rumsfeld had the reputation of being harsh and abrasive in his dealings, so the affable Cheney stepped in and smoothed relations between Rumsfeld and the target of his wrath whenever it occurred. Whether it was the press or another bureaucrat, Cheney had the ability to calm individuals and explain what Rumsfeld's intentions were. Rumsfeld admitted as much when he told one reporter that

Cheney's even temperament enabled Cheney to work with almost anyone.

Cheney benefited from good fortune in 1973, when Rumsfeld accepted the post of ambassador to the North Atlantic Treaty Organization (NATO) in Europe. He asked Cheney to go overseas with him, but his youthful assistant preferred staying in the country. Instead, Cheney accepted a position as vice president of the investment firm, Bradley, Woods, and Company. While retaining his contacts and reputation in government, Cheney distanced himself from the Washington political scene just at the right moment, for Nixon's presidency was about to collapse in light of the Watergate scandal. When President Nixon resigned in disgrace, Cheney avoided any damage to his reputation because he was no longer working for the administration. When a new Republican president, Gerald Ford, stepped in, a scandal-free Cheney was available.

President Ford recalled Rumsfeld from Europe in August 1974 and named him as a top White House adviser. Rumsfeld turned again to his protégé, Dick Cheney, who left

*Cheney resumed working at the White House in 1974 as a deputy assistant to President Gerald Ford and became chief of staff in 1975.*

the investment firm to become a White House deputy assistant. The next year, after Rumsfeld had been named secretary of defense, Cheney succeeded him as President Ford's chief of staff.

Cheney handled an impressive array of responsibilities as chief of staff. He supervised five hundred people, established the president's daily schedule, made sure the heavy flow of memos to and from the president received the proper attention, and gave advice when asked. Fifteen-hour workdays were common, and Cheney earned points for fair-mindedness, friendliness, hard work, loyalty, and an ability to grasp the issues.

Even though he worked at the top level of government, Cheney did not let the stature affect his low-key personality. He drove a ten-year-old Volkswagen to work each day instead of using a chauffeured government limousine, and insisted on being called "Dick."

While working at the White House, Cheney forged close bonds with two other men who would be very influential in his career. Brent Scowcroft, the national security adviser under both presidents Ford and Bush, and James Baker, who would eventually be Bush's secretary of state, spent many hours discussing issues with Cheney. The men would later reunite during the Gulf War.

## Member of Congress

In 1976, Cheney returned to Wyoming following Gerald Ford's loss to Democratic

## Powell's Observations on Cheney

Gen. Colin Powell worked with numerous military and political leaders throughout his career. He thought highly of some, while he disregarded others as weak and ineffective. Dick Cheney fell into the first category, as the following excerpt from Powell's autobiography, *My American Journey*, makes clear.

> Cheney was a cerebral Wyoming cowboy, used to wide-open spaces where one did not have to deal with many people. He was a conservative by nature and in his politics, a loner who would take your counsel, but preferred to go off by himself to make up his mind. And he was supremely self-confident, or the next best thing, he managed to give that impression. Here was someone else who had learned never to let 'em see you sweat. I enjoyed working with a master of the game.

candidate Jimmy Carter in that year's presidential election. He accepted a post in the banking industry, but within two years Cheney was back in politics when he agreed to run for the Wyoming seat in the House of Representatives.

Cheney suffered a major setback during the 1978 election when he was struck with his first heart attack. Within six weeks he had sufficiently recovered to rejoin the campaign trail, but the experience left its mark. As he explained to a reporter, "You become very much aware of your own mortality. When you're 37 years old and you have a heart attack, it's a total surprise. It leads you to question what you're doing and why you're doing it."[34]

Cheney gave up smoking but continued his love affair with hiking and running. The medical affliction did not impede his political ambitions, as Wyoming voters handed him a resounding triumph over Democrat Bill Bagley.

Cheney loved his years in the House of Representatives, where he enjoyed the opportunity to vote on complex issues. During his work in the White House, Cheney spoke for the administration instead of for himself, and he found that somewhat limiting. In the House, he was his own man. He said to the *New York Times* that in the White House "you're ultimately a hired gun. When you serve in the House, you may cast only one of 435 votes, but it's your decision to make."[35]

He described himself as a "compassionate conservative." As such, Cheney frequently voted in favor of prayer in school; a balanced budget; a strong military; aid to rebels in Nicaragua, Afghanistan, and Angola; and against limits on the powers of the president, busing, abortion, and the Equal Rights Amendment. Conservative groups so loved his record that the American Conservative Union gave Cheney a 90 percent approval rating, while the liberal Americans for Democratic Action handed him a mere 4 percent rating. One reporter wrote, "During his decade on the Hill, Cheney was the congressman who never saw a welfare program he didn't hate," or "a weapons system he didn't love."[36]

Cheney exhibited the same loyalty to his Wyoming constituents that he had

given to the president and to Rumsfeld. At one time a large number of congressmen tried to pass legislation allowing their

## Schwarzkopf on Cheney

General Schwarzkopf seemed to hold Cheney in high regard, even though the two had their differences. In his autobiography, *It Doesn't Take a Hero*, Schwarzkopf recalls one of his earliest impressions of Cheney.

> Secretary Cheney had been at the Pentagon just over a year and he'd unnerved a lot of generals by replacing one four-star and giving warnings to others he felt were acting with too much autonomy [freedom]. Yet as I watched and listened to him during the flight [to Saudi Arabia], he impressed me as smart, attentive, and easy to work with.

*Cheney's keen intellect and even temper won the respect of his colleagues.*

states, which suffered in the throes of a devastating drought, to temporarily use some of Wyoming's portion of the mighty Colorado River. They vowed to stop diverting the water once the crisis passed. Cheney defeated the passage, explaining to his aides that once the congressmen succeeded in getting his state's water, they would never relinquish control.

Cheney could remain obstinate when his constituents' interests were involved, but he worked with both Democratic and Republican members in the House with consummate skill. In recognition, fellow Republicans elected Cheney as chairman of the Republican House Policy Committee in his second term, and by 1988 he had risen to the second most important post, the party whip. Wyoming's voters added their vote of confidence by re-electing Cheney to the House of Representatives in 1980, 1982, 1984, 1986, and 1988.

His time in Congress was about to end, though. During one of his meetings, Cheney sat down with senior military advisers to discuss important defense measures. One officer in attendance, Gen. Colin L. Powell, walked away with a favorable impression. Powell later said that Cheney's questions "knifed to the heart of the issue, and I recognized that I was in the presence of an exceptional mind."[37] The two were about to become closely involved in running the nation's military, and in that capacity they would help guide a nation at war.

## Secretary of Defense

On March 9, 1989, White House chief of staff John Sununu asked Cheney if he would accept the position of secretary of defense. When Cheney indicated he would, Sununu asked him the condition of his health in light of his heart troubles. Cheney, who had suffered three mild heart attacks, explained that he had recently undergone a quadruple coronary bypass operation to increase the blood flow to his heart but that it was done more so he could continue his vigorous outdoor activities rather than as a lifesaving mechanism. Cheney's physician had assured him he could remain in government service, hike, and participate in all of the things he had been accustomed to doing.

The next day President George Bush nominated Cheney for the post. Bush later wrote, "I hated to steal from our congressional ranks, but I knew Dick would be accepted on the Hill and would do a great job."[38] Before he received the new assignment, though, a Senate confirmation committee scrutinized Cheney's experience, his views, and his qualifications.

Some wondered why Cheney should receive the important duty when he had no apparent experience in defense. All of his government work had been at the White House or in Congress. Cheney replied that his ten years serving presidents had more than compensated for a lack of work in defense, since he had been required to attend all of the meetings of the National

Security Council, which dealt mainly with military matters.

A bigger issue was Cheney's lack of service in the military. During the Vietnam War he received draft deferments, first as a student and then as a married father of two daughters. This bothered most generals and admirals, although Cheney's deferments had been perfectly legal. When asked by the Armed Service Committee's Senator John Warner about this, Cheney replied, "I basically always complied with the Selective Service System, did not serve, and would have obviously been happy to serve had I been called."[39]

The answer appeared to satisfy everyone for Cheney passed inspection on all counts. On March 17 the Senate approved his nomination, and Cheney became the nation's newest secretary of defense.

Cheney injected fresh air into the military. The nameplate on the door of his Pentagon office was quickly changed from the more formal *Richard B. Cheney* to *Dick Cheney*, and he usually arrived at work wearing his business suit and cowboy boots.

Because the military held doubts about his lack of military background, Cheney felt he had to assert his authority right away. He brought with him his trusted congressional aide, Pete Williams, as special assistant, and surrounded himself with a small group of close friends and advisers with whom he shared his views and discussed key decisions. In his first week, Cheney publicly reprimanded Gen. Larry D. Welch, the air force chief

of staff, for inappropriately discussing sensitive military matters with members of Congress.

Gen. Colin Powell closely observed Cheney and handed him high marks. Powell claimed that Cheney was "incisive, smart, no small talk, never showing any more surface than necessary. And tough. This man, who had never spent a day in uniform, who, during the Vietnam War, had gotten a student deferment and later a parent deferment, had taken instant control of the Pentagon."[40]

He also showed that he possessed a keen grasp of world events and issues. In one of his first memos as secretary, Cheney emphasized the importance of defending the Mideast and its oil supply from any threat, but particularly from Iraq.

Tough decisions awaited Cheney. Because the nation's main adversary of forty years—the Soviet Union—was falling apart due to internal problems, the military no longer needed to be as large as it had been. When President Bush ordered Cheney to trim $10 billion a year from the military budget, the new defense secretary asked the heads of each military branch to submit their ideas on what should be eliminated. Rather than issue dictatorial-style cuts on his own, Cheney impressed the top brass by including them in his decision process. Together, Cheney and the military introduced cuts, such as halting production on certain weapons systems and closing bases, that saved the nation $64 billion over five years.

Cheney's first major international crisis erupted in December 1989 in Panama. The nation's leader, Gen. Manuel Noriega, had been suspected for years of drug trafficking and had squashed talk of democracy in his country. When Noriega's military forces beat up political opponents following one election and threatened U.S. servicemen in that nation, Bush decided he had to act. A military force was dispatched to Panama to secure American installations and free an American held captive.

Cheney sat with other military leaders in Washington, D.C. and listened to the operation's progress as it unfolded. "Cheney

*American soldiers in Panama City during the U.S. invasion of Panama in December 1989.*

sat there that night quietly observing his first war," wrote General Powell. "He kept asking sharp, relevant questions, and every hour or so he moved into the next room to report on a secure hot line to the President."[41]

The experience proved beneficial to Cheney. Within one year he would become involved in another military operation that would make Panama look like child's play.

## The Gulf War

The short but successful Gulf War is where Cheney best illustrated the influence that civilian leaders hold over their

*Cheney provided Powell with all of the supplies necessary to carry out Cheney's plan for a ground assault against the Iraqis.*

own nation's military. Right from the start, Cheney disliked the military plan drawn up by General Schwarzkopf. He and Brent Scowcroft thought the strategy, which called for an invasion into Kuwait straight into the heart of Iraqi defense lines, unimaginative. They mockingly labeled it "hey diddle diddle, straight up the middle" and intended to effect change before the ground action started.

Cheney told Colin Powell, "I have been thinking about this all night. I can't let Norm [Schwarzkopf] do this. I just can't let him do it."[42] He added that the plan could result in American forces futilely smashing into strengthened enemy fortifications and withdrawing with nothing but a high casualty rate.

Instead, Cheney staff members developed what became known as the Western Excursion, a military operation that included a coalition drive straight into Kuwait to hold down Iraqi forces while a second armored force swung around to the west and trapped the Iraqi army from behind. Cheney's ultimate purpose in challenging his own military was to send a message that he wanted tougher action taken against Hussein.

Not surprisingly, both Powell and Schwarzkopf resented what they considered Cheney's interference into military matters, but the secretary of defense believed that he had a duty to hold his subordinates to a lofty standard. Most military observers agreed with his position. By stubbornly rejecting the initial plan and prodding the military to be more creative, Cheney filled his responsibility to have the military answer to government authority.

One of Powell's aides explained, "There was constant friction between Cheney and Powell, which was extremely healthy. Cheney always wanted to do it now. He did not always understand the monstrosity of the buildup. But we probably would not have

been ready as soon as we were if it had not been for Cheney's pressure."[43]

After forcing them to modify plans, Cheney then made sure he handed them the supplies and forces to successfully finish the job. The last thing he wanted was for Powell or Schwarzkopf to complain that they had to go to war with inadequate aircraft, men and women, tanks, and other items. At an October 30 White House meeting, Powell outlined exactly what he required. President Bush and Cheney agreed to every item.

At the same time, Cheney dealt with other nations. In August he traveled to Saudi Arabia to line up support for the American military buildup. He told Saudi leader King Fahd, whose country was threatened by massive Iraqi troop concentrations along their border, that the United States was prepared to send troops to his nation if asked and that the soldiers would remain in his country only as long as needed to repel Hussein. "If you ask us, we will come," said Cheney. "And when you ask us to go home, we will leave."[44] King Fahd immediately agreed to let American soldiers into Saudi Arabia.

Political diplomacy also helped in other ways. While Cheney was not directly involved in the last-minute January 1991 meetings between Secretary of State James Baker and Iraqi foreign minister Tariq Aziz, he believed that they solidified American public support for the war. People liked that up to the final minute, their leaders tried to find a peaceful solution to the problem. When the Baker–Aziz talks collapsed, the nation was more willing to accept a military solution.

A building in Tel Aviv, Israel, shows the destruction caused by Iraqi Scud missiles during the Persian Gulf War.

Cheney quickly handled a difficult situation on the eve of the fighting when the air force chief, Gen. Michael Dugan, spoke too freely to the press about American military intentions in the Mideast. Cheney immediately called the general into his office and ordered him to hand in his resignation by noon that day.

When war began, Cheney continued to influence events. The best example came on the war's second day, when Iraq unleashed a number of missiles, called Scuds, against coalition and Israeli targets. Cheney, Bush, and the other politicians realized that the missiles could bring Israeli retaliation against Hussein, which in turn could bring a more violent Arab reaction against Israel and the United States.

Cheney planned to squash the danger before it reached perilous levels. He spoke to Israeli government officials every day to inform them how many missions had been flown against the missile sites and what the results were. When Cheney was dissatisfied with the number of missions flown against the Scuds, he brusquely ordered an increase. Cheney hated to intervene with the military, but he knew he had to assure Israel of a swift American response. "That's the one place where I intervened really in the conduct of the war,"[45] Cheney later explained.

Some observers worried that Hussein would resort to chemical weapons if conditions appeared desperate. Cheney sent a blunt warning across the ocean. He told reporters, confident that word would reach Iraq through CNN and other news outlets, that the United States possessed a number of ways to respond and that they would consider all options. While he never mentioned nuclear weapons, everyone understood that Cheney had them in mind. As he later explained, "It was deliberately left that vague but obviously somewhat threatening to convey the message to Saddam Hussein that he was much better off if he never, never crossed over that line of actually using chemical weapons against us."[46]

His veiled threat worked. Not once did Hussein turn to his chemical weapons.

In answer to critics who contended that the war ended too quickly, Cheney countered that the American military would have become mired in a drawn-out conflict that no one wanted if it had continued toward Baghdad. The war's objectives—remove Iraq from Kuwait and harm their offensive capabilities—had been accomplished, and the American public did not need at that late hour an expanded war that could produce ghastly American casualties.

Cheney believed that the United States had achieved every purpose. Not only had it halted Iraqi aggression and made a state-

| An Ordinary Guy |
| --- |

Dick Cheney never used the powers of his office to his own benefit, and he did not appreciate it when anyone else did. On one flight to Saudi Arabia with General Schwarzkopf, Cheney twice viewed disturbing occurrences that showed the extent to which some people in high places were willing to go to enjoy the fruits of their offices. He spotted a colonel on the floor of the aircraft ironing one of Schwarzkopf's shirts. Cheney then watched as a long line formed for the lavatory. Instead of standing in line himself, Schwarzkopf ordered another officer to hold a place for him. Cheney could never bring himself to use people in that manner.

ment to nations around the world that it would militarily defend its interests, but the United States had finally put the Vietnam War behind. "The American people were behind the effort in ways we hadn't seen in this country in fifty years. There was this tremendous outpouring of public support, goodwill, restoration of confidence in the military."[47]

## After Desert Storm

Cheney acted as secretary of defense through the remainder of the Bush presidency, mainly overseeing another drastic reduction in the size of the American military. When Bill Clinton took office, Cheney entered the business world to become chief executive of the Halliburton Company. Under his guidance, the company expanded into the largest oil drilling, engineering, and construction services provider in the world.

In August 2000, Republican presidential candidate George W. Bush selected Cheney as his vice presidential running mate. According to initial polls, Bush and Cheney headed toward the November elections with a substantial lead over the Democratic challengers, current Vice President Al Gore and Senator Joseph Lieberman of Connecticut. Cheney resigned his post with Halliburton to devote full time to the campaign, and he and Bush were elected by an extremely close margin.

# Chapter 4

# Tariq Aziz: Iraq's Promoter

**D**uring the Gulf War, most Americans despised the image of Saddam Hussein. Many citizens publicly and privately hoped that the American air assault would include his presidential palace or office so that the dictator would be one of the war's casualties.

The face most frequently seen on television screens by Americans and the voice they most listened to, however, was that of Tariq Aziz, Hussein's minister for foreign affairs. While Hussein remained in the background as an ominous shadow threatening world stability, Aziz stood in front. While the entire world watched, he bargained with the Western powers, appeared on television shows and sat down with newspaper reporters, took heavy criticism on behalf of his ruler, and tried to gain sympathy for Iraq throughout the world. The soft-spoken individual managed to avoid being castigated as a demon, as was Hussein, which was a remarkable accomplishment in view of the heated emotions stirred by the Gulf War.

## Early Life

Tariq Mikhayl Aziz was born in 1936 in the village of Tell Kaif, across the Tigris River from Mosul in northern Iraq, about 225 miles northeast of Baghdad. Like many Iraqi youth of his day, he came from a poor family that inhabited a simple mud hut as a home.

Unlike most Iraqi youth, Aziz did not belong to the dominant Muslim religious group. Instead, he grew up in the Nestorian sect of the Chaldean Catholic Church, a group of people who spoke Aramaic, the language supposedly used by Jesus Christ. While the Chaldeans had been part of the Roman Catholic Church since 1553, they comprised barely 2 percent of Iraq's population and were considered a minority within the Iraqi Christian community. Aziz's Nestorians, a small segment of the Chaldeans, made up even less than that.

Aziz did not go to the same places of worship or follow the same customs as Muslims and consequently found himself on

*Tariq Aziz grew up Christian in Muslim Iraq and often felt excluded by his peers.*

His feelings of separateness and humiliation worsened when his family moved to Baghdad and Aziz started attending school. His father labored as a waiter in a saloon to support the family, a job that others looked down on as menial, and Aziz felt embarrassed that his father did not hold a more respected occupation. While other boys boasted that their fathers worked in offices or in the military, Aziz said nothing.

An Iraqi exile who lived near the young Aziz said he was affected by the harsh treatment of other boys for the rest of his life. The exile told the *London Observer* in 1990 that the harsh treatment made Aziz feel inferior and want to be accepted by everyone. His status as a Christian in a Muslim nation did not help, since Christians were not respected by Iraqi society at large, and Chaldeans were not respected within Christian society. As a result, Aziz searched for a strong man for whom he could work and who would accept him.

Aziz tried not to let his feelings influence his grades. He earned excellent marks throughout elementary and secondary school in Baghdad, then attended Baghdad University's College of Fine Arts. Aziz majored in English literature and graduated in the mid-1950s.

the harmful end of taunts. The bright boy wanted to be accepted, but his religion separated him from the rest. This sense of isolation produced a shy youth who found solace in books and ideas instead of people.

## Early Revolutionary Activity

Aziz taught English literature briefly after graduation, then entered the newspaper business. For a time he was a reporter, then established a reputation and rose to editor of the daily paper, *Al-jumhuriyah* in 1963. During these years Aziz also forged close ties with the outlawed Baath Socialist Party. The organization believed that Arabs, not foreign powers, should determine the future of Iraq, and it intended to replace the British-supported Iraqi government of King Faisal II.

The Baath Party organized attempts to oust different Iraqi governments. In 1956 an abortive attempt against King Faisal forced party members into hiding. Two years later a pro-communist military leader, Abdul Karim Kassem, ousted Faisal, executed him, then ruthlessly hunted down his enemies, especially members of the Baath Party.

When Kassem was overthrown by the Baath Party in 1963, Aziz had high hopes that progress would come to his country. The party remained in power for only ten months, however, before it was replaced by a rival faction. Aziz was critical of Baath Party leadership because he believed that they excluded from positions of influence those poorer members who worked hard to build the party.

Following the coup, the Baath Party split into different groups. Aziz joined an active cell that organized in Tikrit, a town in north-central Iraq. There he met a man from Tikrit who had already established a name in party circles for his revolutionary activity, which included assassination attempts and time in jail. Saddam Hussein and Tariq Aziz fashioned a relationship that lasted through many travails.

Aziz and Hussein had to be patient, for the Baath Party did not return to power until 1968, when Hussein ruled along with Maj. Gen. Ahmed Hassan al-Bakr. Because of his newspaper experience, Aziz was named editor of the Baath Party newspaper.

*Aziz earned a degree in English literature from Baghdad University (pictured).*

For the first time Aziz found himself fashioning the image by which the rest of Iraq and the world would see his cohorts. These years provided valuable experience that he would employ in later years.

Aziz kept moving upward in Baath Party circles. In 1972 he was named a member of the general affairs bureau of the Revolutionary Command Council, which was the governing body of Iraq. Recognizing the talent Aziz possessed in the news profession, President al-Bakr appointed him to the Iraqi cabinet as minister of information in 1974. This promotion made Aziz the only Christian to serve in a Baath Party government. Aziz was given considerable power over the foreign press, including the right to ban literature he felt subversive to the Baath Party. In effect, Aziz became the government's censor of a free press and ideas.

As the government's top propagandist, Aziz was responsible for casting Hussein and al-Bakr in a favorable light. This proved tricky. On the one hand, Aziz could trumpet Hussein's social programs, which emphasized increased literacy and widespread health care for the people. On the other, Aziz had to justify the numerous executions and tortures ordered by Hussein, which earned worldwide condemnation from Amnesty International and other human rights groups. In recognition of his work, in 1977 Aziz was elected as a full member of the party leadership and appointed to the ten-man Revolutionary Command Council. He had gained the ad-miration of many top party officials and was ready to occupy a dominant position once Hussein took full control.

## Strife with Iran

Aziz did not have to wait long. Hussein replaced the ailing al-Bakr as president in July 1979, and quickly named Aziz his deputy prime minister. Aziz continued to be the chief propagandist in the government, attempting to sell the rest of the world on the notion that Hussein cherished nothing more than to help his nation join the community of advanced nations.

## Aziz's Threat

As foreign minister, Tariq Aziz's responsibility was to carry out Saddam Hussein's wishes pertaining to relations with other nations. At times he thus had to be the bearer of hard tidings, as this paragraph describing Aziz's communication with the Arab League from Michael R. Gordon and Bernard E. Trainor's 1995 book, *The Generals' War*, makes clear.

> On July 16 [1990], Tariq Aziz, the Iraqi foreign minister, sent a blistering letter to the Arab League. Even against the backdrop of the ongoing dispute between the Iraqis and the Kuwaitis over boundaries and loan repayments, Aziz's letter was a thunderclap. The Iraqi foreign minister charged that Kuwait's refusal to resolve the border disputes with Iraq, its rejection of Iraqi demands that its multibillion-dollar debt be canceled, and its insistence on pumping oil in excess of OPEC [Organization of Petroleum Exporting Countries] quotas were tantamount to military aggression.

As a close ally of Hussein, Aziz became the target of various assassination plots. The most serious occurred on April 1, 1980, during a speech he delivered to a group of college students. An unknown assailant tossed a bomb toward Aziz, who escaped injury by falling to the ground. When a second bomb exploded four days later, Hussein exacted swift retribution by executing one of his top opponents, Mohammed Bakr Sadr of the pro-Iranian Al Dawa-Al Islam Party and members of his family.

Turmoil with Iran heated to the boiling point with the rise to power of the fundamentalist religious leader Ayatollah Khomeini. The Iranian ruler exhorted followers throughout the Middle East to join him in an Islamic revolution, and he particularly encouraged anti-Hussein dissidents inside Iraq to rebel against their dictator. In 1980 both sides issued threats and moved soldiers to their respective borders. Finally, Hussein opened an offensive in September that seized a huge stretch of Iranian territory.

Hussein added the duties of foreign minister to Aziz's portfolio and assigned him the task of garnering support from Western nations and the rest of the Arab world in his battle against Iranian fundamentalists. Aziz proved to be a mastermind over the next few years. He reestablished ties with Egypt that had been severed in 1978 after Egypt formed relations with Israel. He forged a deal with France to deliver French-built fighter aircraft that could fire the superb Exocet missile, which Hussein used with chilling destructiveness against Iran. He arranged an economic and technological pact with the Soviet Union.

His supreme triumph came with his dealings with the United States. Many Americans castigated Saddam Hussein's government as little more than a reign of terror, but Aziz played on the Americans' greater enmity toward Iran, which had seized a large group of Americans in Tehran and held them hostage for more than one year. He convinced President Ronald Reagan that the greater evil in the Middle East was posed by Khomeini and that Iraq could serve as a buffer to his expansion. For the first time since 1967, during the Arab–Israeli War, diplomatic relations were restored between Iraq and the United States.

When Aziz was later asked by reporters why his nation had been so willing to negotiate with the United States, he answered that he and other leaders had matured as politicians. The response masked reality. Iraq badly wanted to obtain military intelligence on Iran that American spy satellites could hand them, so Hussein agreed to establish relations. American politicians were eager to check Khomeini's advance, so they were willing to deal with Hussein. It benefited both nations to set aside differences and work together.

While Aziz traveled to foreign capitals to construct alliances favorable to Iraq, the war with Iran seesawed. After advancing

*An Iraqi tank crew in 1980. At the outbreak of the Iran–Iraq War, Iraq secured diplomatic relations with the United States in hopes of gaining intelligence information on Iran.*

into Iranian territory, the Iraqi army was thrown back in a determined counteroffensive by Iranian forces. In July 1982 Iran entered Iraq, and for more than two years the opposing armies battled for supremacy. Hussein eventually resorted to chemical weapons, but he succeeded in turning back the enemy only after his soldiers achieved a few triumphs on the battlefield.

In 1987 a weary Iraq agreed to a United Nations–sponsored cease-fire. When Khomeini accepted it the following year, the bloody eight-year war ended. Aziz now had

the duty to negotiate a beneficial truce, and in August 1980 he led a delegation to Geneva, Switzerland, to start peace talks. Aziz stubbornly insisted that Iraq would sign no agreement unless it received a border adjustment to the south guaranteeing it free access to the Persian Gulf. A 1975 treaty fixed that border at a river's midpoint, but Aziz argued the Iraqi border should be extended to the Iranian shoreline. Negotiations stalled over this issue.

Aziz also had to defend Hussein from charges he had used chemical weapons and poison gas. Aziz admitted the Iraqis had turned to chemical weapons during the war but only because Iran had used them first. He heatedly denied that Hussein employed poison gas in his strife with Kurdish rebels in northern Iraq, but television film proved otherwise. When the United States and France called for an international meeting to condemn the use of such weapons, Aziz cleverly asked that the conference also ban the use of nuclear weapons against non-nuclear nations. While on the surface his proposal seemed to make sense, it was actually pointed at archenemy Israel, which supposedly possessed a nuclear arsenal. His crafty ploy gained much praise for Aziz throughout the rest of the Arab world.

## The Gulf War

When Saddam Hussein threatened to disrupt peace in the Middle East because of Kuwait's actions, Aziz again had to face the world's media and government representatives. Aziz claimed that Kuwait's decision to lower the price of oil—which cost Iraq $1 billion each year for every dollar the price of oil dropped per barrel—could not be tolerated, and he declared that the Kuwaiti demand that Iraq repay a war debt was an insult to the memory of the thousands of Iraqis who perished battling the hated Persians. Consequently, in August 1990 the Iraqi army pushed into Kuwait and seized the oil-rich nation.

Aziz had told U.S. secretary of state James Baker in 1989 that Hussein wanted friendly relations with the United States, but when the United States insisted Hussein withdraw from Kuwait, Aziz accused President George Bush of a desire to control the world. He later mentioned in a television interview that Bush "decided to take over the region. He decided to put his hand on the oil reserves. He couldn't do that successfully without destroying Iraq and destroying the military power of Iraq and removing this nationalist, patriotic leadership."[48]

Aziz condemned the United States for organizing what he termed a conspiracy against Iraq and warned the Americans against choosing a military solution. The *New York Times* quoted Aziz in August 1990 as saying, "If the American leader thinks that this is a vacation like that they had in Panama or Grenada [two military operations in the 1980s that unfolded smoothly and quickly for the United States], they are mistaken. It will be a bloody conflict, and America will lose and America will be humiliated."[49]

After President Bush gave Iraq until January 15, 1991 to withdraw from Kuwait, Aziz engaged in a series of diplomatic meetings designed to forestall American action. He traveled to Arab capitals to present Hussein's case and visited Western nations in an attempt to commence negotiations that might avert war. Aziz finally agreed to meet James Baker in Geneva, Switzerland on January 9.

Aziz stated that he did not think the United States had any purpose in agreeing to the meeting other than to win over the American people. He mentioned in a television interview, "I knew that that was public relations. That he [Bush] wanted to tell Congress, 'Look, to the end I tried to find a diplomatic settlement,' so that he could get a few more votes."[50] Saddam Hussein, however, believed that the American willingness to talk indicated a sign of weakness, that the nation had no desire to engage in war and suffer casualties.

Baker and Aziz met for more than six hours but produced little more than dramatic utterances and threats. Baker cau-

## Would Iraq Use Chemical Weapons?

One of the biggest questions faced by President Bush and the other coalition leaders was whether Saddam Hussein would resort to chemical warfare. Though preparations could be made in anticipation, it was not a prospect that any wished to ponder. One Arab viewpoint is expressed in the following excerpt, taken from Khaled bin Sultan's 1995 memoir of the Gulf War, *Desert Warrior*. The general was a member of the Saudi royal family and Saudi military.

> As the ground war approached, a question which had worried us from the beginning was now posed more insistently than ever: would Saddam use chemical weapons? I myself believed he would not dare. He must have known that if he did so an enraged United States would go all out to destroy him, as Secretary of State James Baker made clear to Tariq Aziz, at their abortive meeting in Geneva on January 9. As Saddam's own personal survival was paramount in his mind, I reckoned that the chance of his using such weapons was remote.

*An American soldier wears a protective suit during a chemical warfare exercise in Saudi Arabia in 1990.*

tioned Aziz that Iraq had to withdraw from Kuwait by the United Nations–imposed deadline of January 15 or face severe retaliation. Aziz countered by insisting that any pullback had to be done in conjunction with an Israeli withdrawal from contested lands in other parts of the Middle East. He warned that if the United States was foolish enough to attack Hussein, Iraq would immediately strike Israel.

Aziz shrugged off Baker's contention that Iraq faced opposition and condemnation from most nations in the world. "No, we have a problem with you," he said. "The representative of the international community, the Secretary General of the United Nations is not talking with me now, you are talking with me."[51]

Baker then handed Aziz a sealed envelope containing a letter from George Bush to Saddam Hussein, and a copy of the letter for Aziz to read. The letter stated, in part, that "the American people would demand the strongest possible response" should Hussein remain in Kuwait or order terrorist actions against Americans throughout the world, and that "You and your country will pay a terrible price if you order unconscionable acts of this sort."[52]

Hussein had earlier instructed Aziz to use his judgment about accepting the letter, which they knew was coming with Baker, and Aziz answered that if he thought the letter contained a threat, he would reject it. "I took the letter from him [Baker] and I read it," Aziz later explained. "I read it very carefully and then when I

ended reading it, I told him, 'Look, Mr. Secretary, this is not the kind of correspondence between two heads of state. This is a letter of threat and I cannot receive from you a letter of threat to my President.'"[53]

Baker countered that Hussein perched on the brink of war and that once started, the United States would hurl all its might against Iraq to achieve a fast and decisive end. Aziz replied, "My youngest son is eleven years old. The experiences of his lifetime are exclusively confined to war, to expecting Iranian air raids and missiles. So, war is not something alien to us." He added,

> You are a power which possesses strong weapons. You have your estimates about the effectiveness of these weapons. You have your plans and you are convinced that if you start the war against Iraq you will win and you will smash us. We have a different conviction. I sincerely and without pretension tell you that the nineteen million Iraqis, including the Iraqi leadership, are convinced that if war erupts with you, we will win.[54]

The meeting ended with these bold words. Baker informed a group of reporters later that he saw no willingness from Aziz to discuss peace, and said that now the world could only wait for the January 15 deadline. On January 12, in Washington, D.C., the Bush administration received the support of Congress when the Senate voted 52 to 47 to authorize military

## Bush Contacts Hussein

In one final attempt to avert war, George Bush asked Secretary of State James Baker to deliver a letter to Tariq Aziz in Geneva. The note, written for Saddam Hussein, was handed to the Iraqi foreign minister in January 1991, shortly before the war started. Aziz did not like the letter's contents, which included the following selection, excerpted from George Bush's 1999 book, *All the Best, George Bush.*

> The United States will not be separated from its coalition partners. Twelve Security Council resolutions, 28 countries providing military units to enforce them, more than one hundred governments complying with sanctions—all highlight the fact that it is not Iraq against the United States, but Iraq against the world. That most Arab and Muslim countries are arrayed against you as well should reinforce what I am saying. Iraq cannot and will not be able to hold on to Kuwait or exact a price for leaving.

force, and the House of Representatives approved 250 to 183.

Aziz helped develop resolute intentions in Iraq. He informed the nation that Iraq would never yield to American demands for what he termed an unconditional surrender. Citizens responded to Aziz by demonstrating in the streets, shouting anti-American slogans, and proclaiming that they would rather die than give in to President Bush.

Once the air war opened on January 17, Aziz tried to create a favorable climate for Iraq among other Arab nations. He wrote a letter to the Arab League in which he outlined Iraq's position in regard to Kuwait and asked all Arab lands to unite behind Hussein. He then visited Iran and tried to normalize relations with Iraq's recent foe. Despite Aziz's efforts, though, Iraq remained isolated among the community of nations.

While the devastating air assault left much of Iraq's military capabilities in smoke, Aziz opened negotiations with the Soviet Union in hopes of avoiding a ground war with the U.S.-led coalition forces. He met with Soviet leader, Mikhail Gorbachev, on February 17 and February 22, but the difficulty he encountered in arranging anything that might be acceptable to the United States—short of complete surrender—was illustrated in the route he was forced to take simply to arrive in Moscow. Rather than taking a jet from Baghdad to Moscow, which carried with it the real prospect of being shot down by the American aircraft that controlled the skies, Aziz drove across the Iranian border, hopped on a helicopter to Tehran, then boarded a jet for the Soviet capital. Before any ground assault had opened, the United States had gained such complete supremacy in the air that the nation's foreign minister had to use subterfuge simply to leave the country.

Gorbachev hoped to persuade Aziz that only by a speedy withdrawal from Kuwait could his nation expect an end to the war. Instead of recognizing the reality that his nation was already being militarily manhandled, Aziz issued demands of his own. He wanted UN sanctions on economic goods lifted, and he insisted that any withdrawal from Kuwait be done in slow phases. Gorbachev understood from

talking with American diplomats that this stance would be unacceptable, but he was unable to convince Aziz to soften his demands.

Coalition leaders saw Aziz's moves in Moscow as nothing more than a maneuver to delay the expected ground attack. Few had any patience to continue the diplomatic game any longer. British prime minister John Major, who had succeeded

*Foreign Minister Aziz tried unsuccessfully to garner support for Hussein from other Arab nations.*

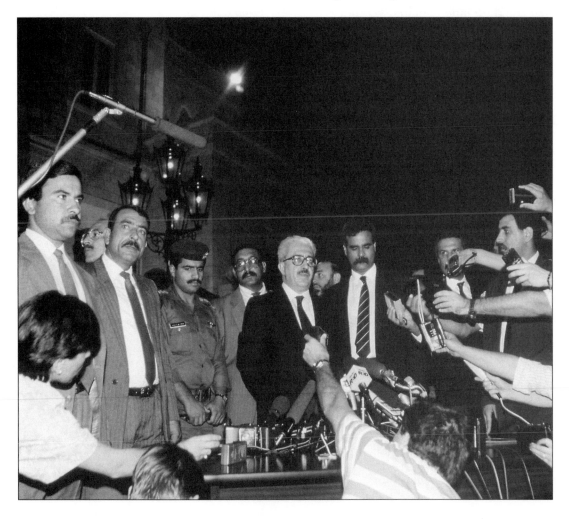

Margaret Thatcher, said, "It's time for [Hussein] to stop fooling about. We are not prepared to be strung along."[55]

Aziz traveled to Moscow with no illusions that he could prevent the ground assault. He was astonished at its swiftness and potency, however. The coalition ground forces demolished much of the Iraqi army in a matter of days. With Kuwait lost and much of Hussein's military might shattered, Aziz could do little to help his country.

Aziz lost the duties of foreign minister in a March 1991 restructuring. He retained his title as deputy premier, however, and remained involved in day-to-day diplomacy. Aziz focused on getting the United Nations to lift its economic sanctions, but since he bargained from a weakened position, the economic woes continued to plague Iraq for much of the decade.

Aziz has survived for so long in the tumultuous Iraqi political world because he knew how to appease Hussein. The crafty politician, who named the youngest of his three children Saddam, immediately realized that to remain in power under Hussein, one had to submit to Hussein's wishes. One Baath Party member explained to the *London Observer*,

His weak point is that he is a yes-man 100 percent. He is a pleasant guy, nice to sit with and have a drink with. He is clever, well-educated, shrewd in hiding his real beliefs. He is a messenger, an expert who speaks very good English. He will tell Saddam what he thinks he wants to hear. This is his character: to say what his superior would like to listen to.[56]

*Iraqi soldiers lie on the ground, casualties of the Persian Gulf War.*

At the same time, Aziz believed that Iraq gained a partial victory from the war with the United States. He knew that the Iraqi army had been defeated, but in the long run he felt that his country had benefited because Iraq gained the admiration of the rest of the Arab world for standing up to foreign powers. As he explained in a television interview, "In our region, when a leadership fights against the Americans, it politically survives. It's not a wrong-doing you see, in the eyes of the Iraqi people, to have a conflict with Israel, or the United States, because of the history of this region."[57]

Aziz remained in office long after the Gulf War ended, trying to weave a positive image for his nation in the face of great hostility. His career provided an excellent example of what a diplomat must do—act in the best interests of his country. Though he represented the tyrannical rule of Saddam Hussein and had to defend the blatant invasion of Kuwait, Aziz was always ready to promote the welfare of Iraq.

# Chapter 5

# Colin Powell: Promoter of the Military

**E**very army needs someone in the background to represent its interests. That individual presents the military point of view to the rest of the population, assembles the material needed to achieve a speedy victory on the battlefield, and provides overall framework for the operation. During the Gulf War, the United States leaned heavily on Gen. Colin Powell to be such a person.

## Early Life

Colin Luther Powell was born in New York City on April 5, 1937, to Jamaican immigrants. Both his father, Luther Theophilus Powell, and his mother, Maud McKoy Powell, worked in the city's garment district and provided a happy, secure lifestyle for Colin and older sister Marilyn.

Powell grew up in a rough section of the South Bronx called Hunt's Point. Burglaries and street fights between rival gangs were common, yet Powell loved the neighborhood for its ethnic diversity and the ten-

dency for the neighborhood families to watch out for each other. Powell's sister, Marilyn, said years later, "We were always closely supervised. When you walked down the street, you had all these eyes watching you."[58]

Powell enjoyed playing baseball and going to the movies with his group of friends. They reenacted World War II battles in area parks, flew model airplanes, and admired military uniforms and their shiny medals.

Powell earned mediocre grades in New York City's public schools. Not until junior high, when he was elected class captain, did he first show the initiative that would later drive him to success. He continued his lackadaisical performance into high school, but he showed strength of character outside of school. He served as an altar boy at his Episcopal church and proved such a valuable employee at a furniture store that the owner promoted him from stock boy to salesman.

Of the group of neighborhood friends, only Powell and one or two others succeeded. Drugs and gangs took the rest. Powell benefited from the love of his parents and their emphasis on staying away from drugs.

Powell entered City College of New York (CCNY) in 1954 with no ideas of what he wanted to be. One day, though, as he walked about the campus he spotted a group of uniformed students marching in precision. When he inquired about the students, he learned that they were part of the college's fifteen hundred cadets in the Reserve Officers' Training Corps (ROTC). Powell joined and forged an instant rapport

*Colin Powell avoided the drugs and gangs common in his neighborhood thanks to the support and encouragement of his parents.*

with the military structure and organization. He wrote later, "The uniform gave me a sense of belonging, and something I had never experienced all the while I was growing up; I felt distinctive."[59]

For the first time in his life Powell committed to something. He still gained average grades in most subjects, but excelled in military courses. By his senior year, Powell had become cadet colonel, the highest rank available to an ROTC student.

Powell graduated from CCNY in June 1958 and was sworn into the U.S. Army. The excited young man set out for three years of duty in the military.

## Into the Army

Second Lieutenant Powell headed to Fort Benning, Georgia, for five months of training in the Infantry Officer Basic Course, where he learned how to command small units of soldiers in battle. He impressed other officers with his natural ability to lead. One soldier said, "One of the things that struck you was his maturity, even at a very young age. He had a sense of confidence about himself that was like an aura."[60] Powell then completed training with the elite Army Rangers, a unit comparable to the navy's SEALs, and in airborne school, where he learned how to parachute.

In 1959 Powell headed to his first overseas assignment, commanding a platoon of forty men in West Germany. His capable leadership gained a promotion to first lieutenant in December 1959.

## The Value of Honesty

An incident that occurred when Powell was in high school had a profound impact on him. One summer he attended a church camp with a group of boys. They sneaked out of camp one night and purchased some beer, which they then hid in the toilet tank to keep cool. Unfortunately, the camp priest discovered the beer and started an investigation. When he assembled all the boys, only Powell stood up to admit his role in the caper.

Powell was sent home and expected to be severely punished by his parents. However, the priest contacted the Powells to explain their son's admirable confession, and his parents let him off with a lecture. In his autobiography, *My American Journey*, Powell wrote "From a juvenile delinquent, I had been catapulted to hero. Something from that boyhood experience, the rewards of honesty, hit home and stayed."

Powell completed his three years of service in 1961 but never considered leaving. He intended to make a career out of the army, which was one of the few institutions in the nation at the time that offered a black man an opportunity to succeed. He mentioned later that because the army instituted a fairer system than any southern city or northern corporation, "The Army, therefore, made it easier for me to love my country, with all its flaws, and to serve her with all my heart."[61]

Shortly before Thanksgiving 1961, Powell met Alma Johnson. He was instantly stricken by her beauty and charm, and the two began seeing each other as frequently as possible. In August 1962, Powell received orders to head overseas to a country with which most Americans were unfamiliar, but which would soon involve the nation in agony—Vietnam. Before leaving, he and Alma were married on August 25, 1962.

The couple lived in North Carolina while Powell attended a training course at Fort Bragg in preparation for being sent into a dangerous location. Though they experienced the sting of bigotry in the southern city, the Powells lived the happy life of newlyweds for four months. Shortly before Christmas 1962, Powell kissed his wife good-bye and headed to Vietnam.

## Service in Vietnam

Powell flew to the remote A Shau valley near the Laotian border, where he would work as an adviser to four hundred South Vietnamese troops who were attacking supply lines flowing from communist North Vietnam to the South Vietnamese communist forces, the Vietcong. Powell participated in lengthy jungle patrols that tried to locate enemy forces but instead encountered dense foliage, leeches, and steamy heat. The boredom was occasionally broken by a Vietcong ambush, but Powell was frustrated that the fighting appeared to have no purpose. The soldiers left for patrol, tried to avoid contact with the enemy, then returned to their base to await another patrol.

On July 23, 1963, Powell trekked through the jungle with a group of soldiers to a nearby camp. As he cautiously stepped forward, the ground gave way and Powell's right foot was impaled by the sharp end of a *punji* stick, bamboo sticks with sharpened points covered with animal dung. Powell hobbled to camp, even though his foot instantly ballooned from the poison spreading through his wound.

Doctors at a hospital in Hue treated the wound, and Powell was able to return to duty a few weeks later. Instead of heading to A Shau, he was assigned to division headquarters in Hue. While there, Powell reacted in disgust to the tendency of American staff officers to paint a rosy picture of the war in their reports. Staff documents claimed that many villages had been secured, but Powell knew from his service in the A Shau valley that this was not the case.

Powell returned to the United States at the end of 1963, where he saw his son, Michael, for the first time. He entered a nine-month Infantry Officer Advanced Course designed to prepare captains for company command, then was selected to attend the army's prestigious Command and General Staff College at Fort Leavenworth, Kansas, an important step for those desiring to rise to top command posts.

Powell headed back to Vietnam in 1968 as executive officer of a battalion serving near Chu Lai. Four months later he was placed on the staff of Maj. Gen. Charles M. Gettys, where he developed operational plans for eighteen thousand soldiers.

Powell earned a soldier's medal for bravery while working for Gettys. On November 16, 1968, Powell and Gettys rode a

helicopter into the jungle to visit troops. As they were landing, the helicopter blades clipped the top of trees and dropped the chopper to the ground with a jarring thud. Powell scampered out of the damaged aircraft, then rushed back to retrieve a badly injured Gettys and three other officers. He accomplished these rescues even though the helicopter could have exploded at any second and despite a broken ankle.

*American soldiers in Vietnam spent much of their time on patrol searching for the enemy.*

Similar to his first tour in Vietnam, Powell was sickened by much of what he saw. The United States lacked an overall strategy. Patrols simply disappeared into the jungle, searched for the enemy for a few days, then returned to camp. Growing antiwar sentiment back home, where college students mounted huge war protests and burned draft cards, demoralized the troops. When Powell returned to the United States in 1969, hostile feelings toward the military dominated the nation. Powell swore that if he ever rose to command large numbers of soldiers, he would not allow them to fight in such a halfhearted manner as had occurred in Vietnam.

## To Washington, D.C.

For the next two decades Powell served in a series of posts that alternated between overseas duty and service in Washington, D.C. During this time he honed his command talents and so impressed top Washington politicians that he became an influential military adviser.

### Bigotry's Ugly Face

Colin Powell fought in the service to protect his country, but because of the color of his skin he was not always able to purchase a simple meal. In 1964 he stopped at a Georgia restaurant to purchase a hamburger. When the waitress asked if he was Puerto Rican or a visitor from Africa, Powell replied that he was an American Negro. As mentioned in David Roth's 1993 biography of Powell, *Sacred Honor*, the waitress replied, "Well, I can't bring out a hamburger [to where white customers eat]. You'll have to go to the back door." A disgusted Powell drove away without the hamburger rather than comply with the humiliating request.

After earning a master's degree in business and being promoted to lieutenant colonel in the early 1970s, Powell worked at the Pentagon, the enormous structure housing the military's highest commanders. In November 1971 he was named as a White House Fellow, a training program designed for only the most capable of military and political newcomers. In this assignment, Powell worked with powerful politicians and journalists and gained valuable experience in the world of Washington politics.

His field commands included service in Korea as top officer of the First Battalion, Thirty-second Infantry; commander of the Second Brigade, 101st Airborne Division in Fort Campbell, Kentucky; assistant division commander of the Fourth Mechanized Infantry Division in Colorado; and commander of the V Corps in Frankfurt, Germany. He excelled at each step by implementing measures designed to improve morale—such as instituting a Soldier of the Month award—and by insisting on thorough training.

When he arrived in Korea, for instance, he learned that his battalion was riddled with drug abuse, racial strife, and low morale. Powell quickly leveled charges against the most serious drug offenders, handed more responsibility to younger officers, and kept the soldiers so busy they would have little time to complain. "We started running them every morning for four miles and working their butts off," Powell explained, "and they were too tired to get in trouble, too exhausted to think about drugs. When nightfall came, they collapsed." [62]

In Washington, Powell worked as a military adviser in the Office of Management and Budget and as an assistant to top leaders in the Defense Department and Energy Department. His most important work during this time occurred when he was named senior military assistant to Secretary of Defense Caspar Weinberger. The two men developed an instant rapport, and Weinberger handed enormous responsibility to

*As a commander, Powell kept his soldiers busy with exercise, training, and responsibility to boost morale and keep them out of trouble.*

the bright officer. Powell coordinated Weinberger's meetings and conferences, decided who got in to see him, and usually traveled with the secretary on his visits around the nation and world.

Powell proved that Weinberger's confidence in him was deserved during the October 1983 U.S. invasion of the tiny Caribbean island of Grenada, where Powell supervised a speedy military operation to ensure the safety of American students attending college on the island. Three years later he helped plan an air attack on Libya after its ruler, Mu'amar Gadhafi, supported acts of terrorism around the world.

His most controversial episode involved the Iran Contra incident in 1985. Some Washington politicians, including high assistants to President Ronald Reagan, ignored the dictates of Congress by sending aid to the Contras, a group of rebels fighting the pro-communist government in Nicaragua. When Powell learned of this, he wrote a memo to Weinberger urging that Congress be notified of the secret dealings. Afterward, an investigation into the dealings implicated a number of officials and led to the removal of the national security adviser, but Powell received praise for writing the memo and was cleared of any involvement.

## Top Levels of Command

Beginning in 1986, Powell occupied high-profile commands. In December of that year President Ronald Reagan asked him to serve as the deputy national security adviser, the top assistant to the individual who consults with the president on all matters of defense and security. People working for Powell liked the manner in which he attempted to build a team concept—he clearly stated each person's responsibilities and insisted that no one operate in secrecy. He wanted everyone to freely present their views, so that when he and the national security adviser traveled to the White House they would be armed with the best recommendations.

Reagan so appreciated Powell's precise work that he appointed Powell as national security adviser in November 1987. In that post Powell successfully coordinated summit meetings between Reagan and Soviet leader Mikhail Gorbachev, and Reagan always knew that he could count on a blunt assessment of any issue, even if the opinion expressed differed from the president's.

As Powell rose through the ranks, he felt a duty to represent African Americans to the best of his ability. In his speeches, he referred to contributions by black soldiers throughout the nation's history.

In 1988 Powell received a promotion to four-star general and was placed in charge of Forces Command near Atlanta, Georgia. In this crucial post, the largest any army general can hold, Powell had the responsibility for the defense of the continental United States. Within five months, however, Powell was on the move again. In October 1989 he became the first African American to be named chairman of the

Joint Chiefs of Staff, the most powerful military position outside of the president.

## Joint Chiefs of Staff

The Joint Chiefs consists of the heads of the army, navy, marines, and air force, presided over by a chairman. They discuss top military policy and make recommendations to the president, who then decides what to do. The fifty-two-year-old Powell was the youngest man to occupy the position and the first chairman not to have graduated from one of the military academies.

Powell had no time to grow into the job. Within two months, a marine had been killed in Panama, and Powell recommended that the United States dispatch military forces to protect American citizens and interests in the country. A December 20, 1989 invasion, called Operation Just Cause, succeeded in removing Noriega from office and bringing him to trial.

Powell's responsibility during the attack was to explain the action's goals to the public. His comfortable style conveyed calm efficiency to the nation, which accepted that the operation was necessary. Powell would soon have to do much more convincing when trouble brewed in the deserts of Kuwait.

In light of the economic and political troubles faced by the Soviet Union, Powell hoped to reduce the American military. He had to postpone his plans, however, when Saddam Hussein sent eighty thousand Iraqi soldiers into Kuwait in August 1990.

While the United States and other nations condemned Iraq's actions and imposed an economic embargo, Powell met with President George Bush to decide what the military response should be. Remembering Vietnam, Powell insisted that the president draw up a clear set of goals for any military operation in the region, and that once decided, the leaders commit to delivering all necessary troops and supplies to quickly finish the job. Powell reminded the president and his advisers that they had to decide whether the ultimate goal was to remove Hussein from Kuwait, or to invade Iraq, seize Baghdad, and drive Hussein from power.

Powell, hoping to avoid bloodshed, argued for time to allow the economic sanctions to work. Other advisers, such as Secretary of Defense Dick Cheney, urged a speedy use of the military and labeled Powell a reluctant warrior. "I think it would be fair to say that he [Powell] was more prepared to sit tight and let sanctions work and I was not as prepared to let sanctions work, didn't have as much confidence in sanctions as he did,"[63] said Cheney.

Powell answered that he was simply presenting all viewpoints for Bush to consider. Once the decision was made, as a dutiful soldier he intended to carry out the orders. Eventually, Bush decided that should war erupt, the goals would be to drive Hussein out of Kuwait and to destroy the Iraqi capability to make war. Powell later wrote, "In none of the meetings I attended was dismembering Iraq, conquering Baghdad, or changing the Iraqi form of government ever seriously considered."[64]

As the days wound by, it became apparent that economic sanctions would not force Hussein to change his plans. In an October 30 White House meeting, Powell turned to the military option and recommended that a coalition of military forces, led by the United States, push Hussein back to Iraq. He proposed an intense bombing attack in January 1991, followed by a ground assault the next month. President Bush accepted the plan and agreed to

issue an ultimatum to Hussein that he either remove his military from Kuwait by January 15, 1991, or face severe repercussions.

Powell's next step was to organize the many military units and material and get it to Saudi Arabia as quickly as possible. A mere five days after the first Iraqi soldier stepped onto Kuwaiti soil, the initial American contingent landed in Saudi Arabia,

*When Iraq invaded Kuwait, Chairman of the Joint Chiefs of Staff Powell favored the economic sanctions over an immediate military response.*

and from then until January an amazing buildup continued. Again drawing from lessons learned in Vietnam, Powell assembled an overwhelming force so that American men and women would not have to fight a protracted war and risk losing support back home. Powell agreed to a larger number of troops than even Gen. Norman Schwarzkopf, the American commander on the scene, requested. "We had paid for this stuff," wrote Powell in his autobiography. "Why not use it? What were we saving it for? Go in big, and end it quickly. We

*Powell advocated sending large numbers of troops in order to end the conflict as quickly as possible.*

could not put the United States through another Vietnam."[65]

## The War Begins

The January deadline passed without any indication from Hussein that he intended to pull out of Kuwait. As a result, Instant Thunder was put into effect. On January 17, waves of coalition aircraft bombarded Iraqi radar sites and other crucial military targets, and they continued their assaults over the next month.

Powell took a leading role in spreading information to the public. He constantly emphasized to subordinates the value of maintaining good relations with the media, else you could win a fight on the battlefield but lose it on the nation's television screens. To gain the public's support, he repeated in press conferences, "Our strategy to go after this army is very, very simple. First, we're going to cut it off, and then we're going to kill it."[66]

He also excelled at developing a smooth-functioning team among the various military branches. The army, navy, marines, and air force pushed their own agendas, and Powell made sure their views were heard. When a decision was made, he carefully explained the reasons to the heads of each branch. For instance, the air force argued that it could win the war alone, but Powell realized that a ground attack would also be required. He convinced President Bush of this, then smoothed any ruffled air force feathers.

American ground forces crossed into Kuwait on February 24. They advanced so speedily against dispirited Iraqi opposition that in some places American units moved sixty miles in one day. By the fourth day the Iraqi army was in complete disarray and all major objectives had been accomplished. Powell, Bush, and Schwarzkopf conferred, and rather than risk more death decided to end the war at midnight of the fourth day.

Controversy arose that the war had ended too soon. Hussein remained in power in Baghdad, and many Iraqi army units escaped to fight another day. Powell and others countered that the goal had never been to remove Hussein or occupy Iraq. They had been ordered to force Iraq out of Kuwait, which they accomplished, and destroy Iraq's ability to wage war. Powell claimed they had also achieved that goal, but other military analysts disagreed.

The American people joyously greeted the victorious conclusion to the war. Parades filled the streets of Washington, D.C.,

## The Vietnam Effect

All military leaders and most political officials recognized the specter that Vietnam posed during the Gulf War. A speedy victory was sought, a mighty military machine was assembled, and the power of television was recognized. Military analyst Rick Atkinson explained one incident during a television documentary that aired on Public Broadcasting System (PBS).

Dover Air Force Base, which is the main mortuary for the U. S. military, quadrupled in size in anticipation that there would be this flood of casualties coming through. And yet it was quite sealed off from the press. There was concern that televised images of forklifts unloading the American war heroes coming home dead from the battlefield would knock the pins out from under support for the war faster than anything Saddam Hussein could do otherwise.

Chicago, and New York City, and Congress authorized money for a special medal to honor Powell. The warm reaction heartened career soldiers like Powell and Schwarzkopf who remembered the bitter welcome during Vietnam.

## After the War

Now that the crisis in the Mideast had been settled, Powell turned to the other major issue confronting him—the reduction of the U.S. military. As long as the Soviet Union existed and threatened American interests, a huge military machine had to be put into the field. With its dissolution, however, Powell could not justify keeping large numbers of soldiers in uniform.

In February 1992 he recommended to President Bush that he adopt the Base Force notion. If accepted, the United States would always maintain enough military

*After his 1993 retirement Powell spent his time traveling around the country delivering speeches and working with young people.*

strength to simultaneously fight two major regional conflicts. The president agreed, and later in the year the reduction started.

Powell received heavy criticism for his stand on another sensitive issue—the existence of gays in the military. Powell believed that they should be forbidden to join because the military required men to live and sleep in close quarters. He thought the presence of gays would be upsetting to non-gays.

Commentators castigated Powell for his stance and wondered how an African American could support a policy that denied rights to any group of people. He answered that civil rights and admittance of gays into the military were two separate issues—one was an issue of skin color and the other of sexual orientation.

After thirty-five years in a uniform, Colin Powell retired from the military in September 1993. He signed a profitable deal to write his memoirs, which ap-

peared in 1995 as *My American Journey*, and delivered speeches around the country. He was especially interested in reaching the nation's youth, whom he targeted with written and spoken exhortations to work hard, have a dream, and never give up. He also became heavily involved with America's Promise, an organization that assists young people in career education, health, and community involvement.

Powell's name was frequently mentioned as a presidential nominee, but he decided in November 1995 not to run. He wanted more time with his family, and he and his wife were concerned over the lack of privacy that a public office brings. "To be a successful politician requires a calling that I do not yet hear," he later wrote. "I believe that I can serve my country in other ways, through charities, educational work, or appointive posts."[67]

# Chapter 6

# H. Norman Schwarzkopf: Commander

**S**ince the Vietnam War, American military leaders understood the importance of having the support of the nation for any military endeavor. In some ways, the United States lost the war on the battlefields of Vietnam because the effort failed to win the war for popular support back home. Men who had experienced that harsh lesson promised not to let it occur again. One of those individuals rose to command the coalition forces in the Gulf War.

## Early Life

H. Norman Schwarzkopf was born on August 22, 1934, in Trenton, New Jersey, to Ruth Bowman and (H.) Herbert Norman Schwarzkopf (his father gave him only the initial H. because he so hated his own name Herbert). His mother supervised nurses at a local medical center, while his father compiled a distinguished career in the military, in police enforcement, and on the radio. For a time in the 1930s he hosted

the popular *Gangbusters* radio show, in which he interviewed people involved in solving crime.

His father loved West Point and the military. He was honored to have graduated from the academy and served his nation, and he tried to impart that sense of duty to his son. "From the first day I could remember, my parents had told me I was going to West Point,"[68] recalled Schwarzkopf years later.

In 1942, when his father left for overseas duty in World War II, he handed Norman his cherished West Point sword, which was considered a sacred item in the Schwarzkopf home. "I'm placing this sword in your keeping until I come back," he told the eight-year-old youth. "Now, son, I'm depending on you. The responsibility is yours."[69]

Young Norman received a superb education, attending mainly private academies or living overseas with his father at foreign government posts in the Mideast and in

Europe. He learned to speak fluent German and French in European schools, and received his first military discipline at Bordentown Military Institute near Trenton and at Valley Forge Military Academy in Wayne, Pennsylvania.

Norman was determined to follow in the footsteps of his father, who eventually rose to the rank of brigadier general. When the ten-year-old posed for a class picture at Bordentown, he adopted a determined look. As he explained to classmates, "Someday when I become a general, I want people to know that I'm serious." [70]

The athletic Schwarzkopf earned a football scholarship to attend West Point. While there, he also participated in wrestling, tennis, and singing in the choir, and performed well enough in the classroom to graduate 43rd in a class of 480 in 1956.

The other cadets, who nicknamed Norman "the Bear" or "Stormin' Norman" because of his temper, recognized his leadership talent and ambition. Retired general Leroy Suddath, one of Norman's roommates, explained that Schwarzkopf "saw himself as a successor to Alexander the Great, and we didn't laugh when he said it. Norman would predict not only that he would lead a major American

army into combat, but that it would be a battle decisive to the nation." [71] In recognition of his skills, Schwarzkopf was named cadet captain, the highest rank possible at West Point.

*Even as a child Norman Schwarzkopf knew he wanted to become a general.*

## His Mother's Influence

The impact of Schwarzkopf's father on him has been well documented. What is not as commonly known is his mother's influence. Though she suffered from alcoholism, his mother imparted important lessons to her son. General Schwarzkopf relates one incident in his 1992 autobiography, *It Doesn't Take a Hero.*

My father taught me honor, but I learned tolerance from her. While I was on my way home one afternoon, a black lady who had been our maid got on. I had been taught that when a lady gets on a bus, you offer her your seat. So I gave her mine, but some kids started snickering and whispering as though I had done something really dumb. When I got home, I told this to Mom. She stopped what she was doing, sat me down opposite her in the breakfast nook, and told me what I'd done was right. Then she said, "You have to understand that you're one of the luckiest people in the world. You were born white, you were born Protestant, and you were born American. That means you'll be spared prejudices that a lot of other people have to put up with. But always remember: you had nothing to do with the fact that you were born that way. It gives you no right to look down on anybody who wasn't. No matter what the other children say, you must never look down on anybody."

After graduation Schwarzkopf was commissioned a second lieutenant and assigned to Fort Benning, Georgia, for infantry and airborne training. He then served two years with the 101st Airborne Division at Fort Campbell, Kentucky, two years in Berlin, and three years attending various military and engineering schools. In 1964 he received a master's degree in guided missile engineering, then headed to West Point, where he was scheduled to teach for three years. Instead, a major conflict in Southeast Asia interrupted his plans.

## Tours of Duty in Vietnam

As a career officer, Schwarzkopf knew that combat duty was essential for his advancement, so after teaching one year at West Point, he applied for service in Vietnam. He was permitted to go with the stipulation that he complete his three years teaching when the tour ended.

In the summer of 1965 Schwarzkopf, now a major, arrived in South Vietnam to act as a field adviser to a South Vietnamese airborne division in its battles against the communist forces of the Vietcong and the North Vietnamese. Instead of remaining safely in headquarters far from the fighting, as staff advisers did, Schwarzkopf wore the uniform of the South Vietnamese, lived in the jungles with them, ate the same food, and shared the same dangers.

Shortly after his arrival, Schwarzkopf participated in the siege at Duc Co, a tiny outpost in the northern one-third of the country manned by four hundred South Vietnamese and twelve American advisers. Schwarzkopf accompanied patrols into the jungle to locate the enemy, earning a Silver Star medal for bravery after exposing himself to danger to rescue wounded soldiers. In February 1966 he earned another Silver Star for directing fire on a Vietcong stronghold.

Schwarzkopf loved his year in Vietnam. He felt that he had helped the South Vietnamese soldiers become better

fighting men, and he believed that he was doing something worthwhile. He later said,

After my first tour, I came home with probably the greatest feeling of satisfaction I've ever had in anything I've ever done. I slept in the mud, ate rice and Vietnamese food with chopsticks for one solid year. Everywhere the Vietnamese went, I went. I was one of them. And I felt, I really felt I was honestly helping people. [72]

A photo dated August 18, 1965, shows Schwarzkopf leading a column of South Vietnamese soldiers on a march toward Pleiku in central Vietnam.

Schwarzkopf returned to West Point to teach mechanical engineering for another two years. One fall weekend he met a twenty-six-year-old flight attendant named Brenda Holsinger at a football game, started dating her, and within three weeks asked her to marry him. On July 6, 1968, the two were married in the chapel at West Point, shortly before he was promoted to lieutenant colonel and enrolled at the Command and General Staff College at Fort Leavenworth, Kansas.

In December 1969 Schwarzkopf headed back for a second stint in Vietnam, this time as commander of a battalion in the AmeriCal Division. Schwarzkopf again showed great courage under fire, but unlike his first tour, his year in combat produced controversy. On February 18,

1970, an American artillery shell exploded directly above one of Schwarzkopf's units and killed Sgt. Michael Mullen. The sergeant's parents blamed Schwarzkopf for this unfortunate incident and accused him of trying to cover up the incident. Author C. D. B. Bryan wrote a book about the affair and concluded that Schwarzkopf was not responsible, but the incident stirred up antiwar feelings on the home front and caused Schwarzkopf much anguish.

Three months later some of Schwarzkopf's men wandered into a minefield in the Batangan Peninsula, where their unit commander was badly wounded in an explosion. The other soldiers froze in their tracks, afraid to take a step lest they trigger another mine. Schwarzkopf helicoptered to the position to calm the frightened young soldiers and calmly told them to turn back and walk out of the field along the same path they used to enter, but he could see that fear had almost immobilized them.

As Schwarzkopf later recalled, the "other guys started to yell: 'Oh, my God! We're in the middle of a minefield! We're all gonna die!'" When another explosion badly wounded a soldier, Schwarzkopf, shaking in every limb, took the initiative.

I started through the minefield, one slow step at a time, staring at the ground, looking for telltale bumps or little prongs sticking up from the dirt. My knees were shaking so hard that each time I took a step, I had to grab my leg and steady it with both hands before I could take another. I had to nearly double over to move. It seemed like a thousand years before I reached the kid.[73]

Although another land mine killed three more Americans, Schwarzkopf safely removed the injured man and the rest of the unit. For his bravery, Schwarzkopf received his third Silver Star.

Schwarzkopf returned to the United States with a far different feeling than after his first tour. Cynicism and doubt replaced the sense of pride, for he saw much that worried him in Vietnam. Officers remained to the back areas, away from the fighting, or rode in helicopters and directed battle from above, rather than share the dangers with their men. Politicians in Washington, D.C., did not seem to follow a predetermined plan for

## Temper, Temper

Norman Schwarzkopf's temper is legendary, but he rarely carries a grudge against anyone. Once he vents his feelings, Schwarzkopf generally allows the situation to calm.

Col. Burwell B. Bell, Schwarzkopf's executive officer, explained that Schwarzkopf has a full range of emotions. He can get very, very angry, but it's never personal. He's extremely tough on people when it's necessary to get them to do something, but the next minute he'll throw his arm around their shoulders and tell them what a great job they're doing.

conducting the war, and as a result young men in the rice fields of South Vietnam went into battle without a sense of purpose. Finally, the growing antiwar movement back in the United States took its toll on the belief that the nation supported its military.

Schwarzkopf knew that some soldiers had been called baby-killers and spat upon when they returned to the United States.

> I'd made up my mind even before coming home that I'd punch out anybody who spat upon me. Luckily, no one did. But one day that fall, I stopped at a mall in Virginia after work wearing my green uniform. I walked into a department store, and salespeople and other shoppers glared at me. I paid and left as quickly as possible, but getting into the car I thought, "I am in the nation's capital, wearing the uniform of the United States Army, and the people around me see me as some kind of monster!"[74]

Schwarzkopf pondered the lessons from Vietnam and concluded that never again would he fight in a war that had no clear objectives or lacked support from home. He also vowed that if he were in charge, he would bring every ounce of power to bear on the enemy to end the war as quickly as possible so as to avoid the drawn-out Vietnamese conflict that so tore apart the United States.

## Up the Chain of Command

Over the next fifteen years Schwarzkopf occupied a series of posts as he rose through the ranks. He commanded soldiers in Alaska, Germany, and the continental United States, as well as worked on the staff of important Pacific and Washington, D.C., command centers. In 1983 he was promoted to general and given command of the Twenty-fourth Mechanized Infantry Division at Fort Stewart, Georgia. In this post, he participated in the October 1983 U.S. invasion of Grenada. As commander of all ground forces involved in the action, Schwarzkopf gained his first experience commanding large numbers of men in the field.

He gained more experience in 1989 as head of the U.S. Central Command at MacDill Air Force Base in Tampa, Florida. Now a four-star general, Schwarzkopf was responsible for protecting the interests of the United States in the Mideast, and he believed that sooner or later something of significance would occur in that region.

In late July 1990 he and his top commanders formulated a war game based on the premise of Saddam Hussein's Iraqi army invading Kuwait. He very carefully constructed an American response to such an eventuality, then put his forces through an exercise based on the plans. Schwarzkopf's timing proved apt, for within three weeks the Iraqi army dashed into Kuwait and seized its oil fields. The early stages of the Gulf War had begun, with Schwarzkopf already prepared.

## The Gulf War

On August 2, 1990, Iraqi troops stormed into Kuwait and ignited the Gulf War. Schwarzkopf, armed with field-tested plans, immediately began moving American forces into the region. Within five days Operation Desert Shield, the program to transfer vast numbers of coalition soldiers into Saudi Arabia, was put in motion.

An incredible buildup occurred. Between early August and the following January, Schwarzkopf supervised the placement of 750,000 troops and thousands of aircraft and tanks. Making his task more complex was that these men

*Iraqi soldiers during the Iran–Iraq War. Events in the Mideast in the 1980s led Schwarzkopf to anticipate the Iraqi invasion of Kuwait in 1990.*

and women came from different members of the coalition, and Schwarzkopf had to ensure that every country felt its needs were being met. He could not afford to offend a member nation by an inappropriate comment or action.

When neither a trade embargo imposed on Iraq nor the existence of three-quarters of a million troops appeared to sway Hussein, the military option seemed more probable. In meetings with President Bush and top civilian leaders, Schwarzkopf advised that they not turn too quickly to force, but explore every alternative. Consequently, some critics labeled him a weak military leader who shrank from committing soldiers to battle.

Schwarzkopf responded to this by explaining,

I don't consider myself dovish [favoring peace]. And I certainly don't consider myself hawkish [favoring war]. Maybe I would describe myself as owlish—that is, wise enough to understand that you want to do everything possible to avoid war—that once you're committed to war, [you are] then ferocious enough to do whatever is necessary to get it over as quickly as possible in victory.[75]

## The Classic Commander

A military commander has many responsibilities, and one in which Schwarzkopf appeared to excel was in coordinating the efforts of such a diverse coalition. Another military man who understood the hazards of such an undertaking, Colin Powell, describes Schwarzkopf's contributions in this area in his 1995 autobiography, *My American Journey*.

Leading such a diverse force presented a challenge not unlike that which General Eisenhower faced as Supreme Allied Commander in Europe during World War II. Every country involved in the Gulf was sovereign and wanted assurances as to how its forces would be used. Very possibly, Norm Schwarzkopf's greatest single achievement was his extraordinary ability to weld this babel of armies into one fighting force, without offending dozens of heads of states.

Schwarzkopf was also a master at getting along with his Arab hosts. He had lived in the region as a young man and was a serious student of Arab culture. Big, profane Norm could sit and drink tea with Arabs and exchange courtesies for hours with the best of them.

*Schwarzkopf united an international coalition of forces against Iraq.*

When Schwarzkopf submitted his specific plan of attack against the Iraqi army, President Bush, Secretary of Defense Dick Cheney, and others castigated him for being too conservative. He at first intended to send the bulk of the American military directly into the middle of the Iraqi defense lines. Bush believed the unimaginative plan could send hundreds, if not thousands, to their deaths, and with Dick Cheney's urging, he ordered Schwarzkopf to come up with a second plan.

Based largely on the work of Dick Cheney's staff, Schwarzkopf's revised attack plan called for a marine assault into Kuwait to tie down Iraqi forces, an amphibious as-

*Overwhelmed by the magnitude of the coalition forces' ground assault, many Iraqi troops surrendered.*

sault along the coastline to draw more Iraqi troops east, and a swing to the west by three hundred thousand troops to trap the Iraqi army in Kuwait and southern Iraq.

Schwarzkopf may have encountered criticism of his military plans, but at least he obtained from the politicians a clear-cut statement of goals for the war. President Bush outlined that the military was to force the Iraqi army out of Kuwait and to so reduce the military might of Saddam Hussein that he would pose no threat in the foreseeable future.

Schwarzkopf realized that war was imminent when he watched Iraqi foreign minister Tariq Aziz leave the Geneva, Switzerland, meeting with American secretary of state James Baker. Aziz, he said,

walked to the microphones, and droned on for forty-five minutes—without once mentioning Kuwait. I realized this was it: we were going to war. I felt sick at heart as I conjured the terrible risks we were about to face. We knew we would win, but we had no idea what our casualties would be, how the American public would react, or even whether the coalition would hold together.[76]

In the final analysis, Schwarzkopf would be held accountable in each area.

The ground attack went smoothly, in large measure because Schwarzkopf so admirably coordinated a grand deception to shift three hundred thousand troops from the east to the west. Schwarzkopf created an electronic army that sent fake radio signals to and from fictitious units, had trucks in the eastern sector drive at night playing recordings of tank noises, and erected inflatable dummies of vehicles, all designed to trick Iraq into thinking that mechanized units remained in the east. Instead, the troops were pulling out to the west.

When coalition ground forces began their assault, they immediately discovered that the Iraqi army was no match. Taken completely by surprise, Iraqi soldiers surrendered in large numbers. The war unfolded so smoothly that Schwarzkopf moved up the western attack by one day and sent the VII Corps, under command of Gen. Frederick Franks, deep into Iraq to trap the elite Iraqi Republican Guard. When Franks did not move quickly enough, Schwarzkopf exerted his command prerogative and chewed out his subordinate to speed up the attack.

Franks was not the only man to shudder under the wrath of the 6-foot, 3-inch, 240-pound Schwarzkopf. General Powell claimed that "Norm Schwarzkopf, under pressure, was an active volcano. I occasionally found myself in transoceanic shouting matches with him that were full of barracks profanity."[77]

Schwarzkopf showed in other ways how a military commander affects the progress of a war. His temper masked a genius for administering the massive undertaking. He dished out words of praise as freely as his caustic comments, and asked no one to do anything that he could not accomplish himself. One British commander admitted, "Initially we were taken aback by his gung-ho appearance, but in a very short time we came to realize that here was a highly intelligent soldier—a skilled planner, administrator and battlefield commander."[78]

He not only held the coalition nations together, but dealt skillfully with the press. Though some in the media balked at Schwarzkopf's refusal to allow every reporter to travel with troops—he permitted a press pool of selected individuals to go in the field—most found Schwarzkopf willing to share information.

Schwarzkopf used his press conferences to sell the war not only to the press, but to the American public watching on television. He intended to avoid repeating the mistake of Vietnam, where the American military fought without the support of a large number of Americans, so in his press conferences he was informative, blunt, honest, and humorous. Americans warmed to his friendly style and trusted him when he said that the war would soon be over.

One time a reporter asked Schwarzkopf to evaluate Saddam Hussein's talent as a military leader. While many commanders and politicians might have sought a soft answer that stated little, Schwarzkopf replied with a hearty, "Ha! He is neither a strategist, nor is he schooled in the operational art, nor is he a tactician, nor is he a general, nor

is he a soldier. Other than that, he is a great military man."[79]

With his assurance, bravado, and straight talk, Schwarzkopf did much to ensure that the American fighting man and woman received support at home. This translated into increased confidence on the battlefield and helped lead to a speedy victory.

The win came much faster than anyone anticipated. When the Iraqi army crumbled, President Bush decided to end the carnage to avoid charges of continuing what might be seen as needless destruction. When Powell called Schwarzkopf to ask for his opinion on ending the war, Schwarzkopf agreed that since every goal—kicking Iraq out of Kuwait and smashing Hussein's military might—had been achieved, he saw no purpose in sending more Americans into battle.

Schwarzkopf's triumph came at a much lower cost than expected—less than 150 Americans killed and 330 wounded. Schwarzkopf later said, "The loss of one human life is intolerable to any of us who are in the military. But I would tell you that casualties of that order of magnitude is almost miraculous as far as the light number of casualties. It will never be miraculous for the families of those people, but it is miraculous."[80]

Military analysts concluded that Schwarzkopf deserved credit for winning the war and for holding together such a vast coalition of nations. They admitted that he wielded enormous power over Iraq, but as

one said, "The bottom line was Schwarzkopf was given a job and he did it."[81]

*Schwarzkopf (left) declares the terms of surrender to Iraqi officers at the end of the Persian Gulf War.*

## After the Gulf War

Unlike his homecoming following Vietnam, Schwarzkopf returned as a hero. An official welcoming on May 5, 1991, drew twenty-eight thousand people to Tampa Stadium. Three days later the general addressed both houses of Congress and received standing ovations. The next month he led the largest military parade in the United States since the end of World War II in Washington, D.C., then flew to New York City for a massive ticker tape parade nor-

mally reserved for heroes such as Charles Lindbergh and John Glenn. Even the queen of England joined the celebrations by knighting the general.

The only negative moment occurred when Schwarzkopf granted a television interview with reporter David Frost. During the course of the chat, Schwarzkopf stated that he recommended to Bush that he not halt the war so that American forces could plunge deeper into Iraq. When Colin Powell heard these remarks, he reacted angrily. Powell confronted Schwarzkopf and demanded to know if he meant what he said. Schwarzkopf backed down and later reiterated for the press that he had fully supported the decision to end the war.

Shortly before leaving Saudi Arabia, Schwarzkopf talked with Powell about what his new responsibilities might be. Powell explained that Schwarzkopf could take a different command, but he recommended that the general retire. With his immense popularity as a war hero, he would never again enjoy such a position from which to negotiate. Powell mentioned that Schwarzkopf would receive all sorts of lucrative offers. "Now is the perfect time for you to retire. You've been away for a long time. You don't realize what's going to happen when you come home. You're a national idol. People are going to go crazy over you.

You'll be getting all kinds of offers. Now's the time to leave."[82]

Schwarzkopf thought the matter over for a few days, then decided to take Powell's advice. After retiring on August 31, 1991, Schwarzkopf considered the stack of offers. One institution wanted him to be its football coach. Another university sought him as chancellor. Republicans and Democrats inquired whether he would be willing to run for office, and scores of firms offered top executive positions to the general.

Schwarzkopf settled on communications. After writing his autobiography, for which he received $5 million, Schwarzkopf traveled the nation delivering lectures to colleges, civic groups, and military institutions. He worked as a military and political analyst for television, and hosted history documentaries. He may have officially retired from the army, but the military was still a large part of Norman Schwarzkopf.

# Chapter 7

# Charles Horner: Lessons from the Past

**A**ir force general Charles A. Horner's career typified that of most pilots. After developing a love for flying, Horner entered the military, flew in combat during the Vietnam War, and steadily rose through the ranks. Like most military men of his generation, Horner was disturbed by the loss in Vietnam and by what he considered numerous mistakes made by politicians and military leaders. When trouble brewed in the Middle East, Horner's actions as commander of the air arm were heavily influenced by what he saw in Vietnam.

## Early Life

Born on October 19, 1936, in Davenport, Iowa, Horner made little impact on his teachers. The active youth preferred sports or playing with friends to hitting the books.

One passion he developed by the time he was in fourth grade was for pilots and aircraft. Like many boys during World War II, Horner avidly read about the exploits of

famous fliers like marine aviator Gregory "Pappy" Boyington or army flier Jimmy Doolittle. He could even count a pilot among his own family, since his cousin Bill Miles flew a bomber in Europe.

In 1944 Horner learned that flying holds danger as well as fascination. He walked into his house after school to find his mother in tears after receiving news that Miles had been killed while flying a mission over Italy.

For a time he put his thoughts of aviation on hold. After compiling an undistinguished scholastic record in high school, Horner attended the University of Iowa. Friends knew they could usually find Horner wherever a group had gathered to down a few beers or organize a party. In spite of the infrequent hours spent studying, Horner struggled to maintain a C average.

One of the reasons he could not devote his complete attention to study was a diversion by the name of Mary Jo Gitchell.

*Charles Horner developed an interest in aviation as a boy during World War II.*

Horner had known Gitchell in high school, but the two did not start dating until college. They fell in love and began making plans for a life together.

They had to settle one area first. In those days the university required that each male student enter the Reserve Officers' Training Program (ROTC), a college precursor to regular military duty. Horner joined the air force program, where his fascination with aviation blossomed into a full-blown love affair. He told Mary Jo that he wanted to make the military his career, but to be successful, Mary Jo would have to understand that flying would become all-consuming and that she would have to share her life with it. Horner and his future bride agreed that she would never object to his aviation career, and in return he would hand over control of the finances to her. The two married on December 22, 1958, in the Congregational Church in Cresco, Iowa.

## Before Vietnam

On June 13, 1958, a few days before graduation from the University of Iowa, Horner was commissioned in the air force as a second lieutenant. The following October he attended preflight training in Texas, then traveled to Georgia for the arduous primary flight training. Only one in five trainees successfully completes both programs and earns his wings, but for the first time Horner was faced with something he badly wanted. He studied hard, and each night he sat in a chair at home—his makeshift aircraft—and went through the next day's entire flight maneuvers in his head.

After earning his wings in June 1959, Horner spent the next eighteen months in the jet training program at Laredo Air Force Base, Texas, and in gunnery training in Arizona and Nevada. He then received his first assignment, which was a three-year posting at Lakenheath, England, as a fighter pilot with the 492nd Tactical Fighter Squadron.

It did not take long for Horner to see evidence that flying can quickly end a person's life. During his first three months in England, six aircraft crashed and four pilots were killed in accidents.

Two years later he almost died. As Horner piloted an F-100D Super Saber jet over the skies of North Africa, he noticed something approaching from his right. He pulled back hard on his stick to change course and narrowly missed crashing into another American jet that sped by, but the action sent his aircraft into a dreaded stall. With a dead engine, Horner's aircraft plummeted toward the desert thirty-five hundred feet below.

*Horner joined the air force in 1958 and dedicated himself to his studies and flight training.*

Horner knew that many pilots failed to recover from stalls and plunged to their deaths, but he did everything he could think of to regain control. Finally he remembered another pilot explaining how he had pulled out of a spin by simply restarting the engine. Horner did not think it would work because his aircraft was twisting and turning out of control, but fortunately the jet kicked back to life and Horner leveled out just in time.

Horner later explained that he did not think he had a chance to escape death on a day he considers as a turning point in his life. "Every day of my life after that event has been a gift," says Horner.

I was killed in the desert of North Africa. From then on I had no ambition in terms of what course my life was going to take. That was up to God to decide. I'd go do the best I could. I'd enjoy whatever promotions, pay, money that came my way, but I wouldn't live for it. The fact that I made general is no big deal. It's what God wanted me to do, not what I wanted to do. So I gave up me. I let go of my life and everything else in 1962. When I really start getting upset about something, I just say, "The heck with it, I'm dead, it doesn't matter."[83]

Horner returned to the United States for duty at Seymour Johnson Air Force Base in North Carolina in 1963 and then left for duty in Turkey in 1964. While there,

Horner suffered a tragic loss when his parents, his sister Mary Lou Kendall, her husband Bill, and their three children were killed in a car accident in Iowa near Christmas 1964. The shaken Horner flew home for the funerals, then took a short leave to help surviving family members cope with the losses and to deal with his personal grief. Before long, though, he returned to his post and his military duties.

Death became a more dominant feature in June 1965 when Horner received his next posting. He was ordered to temporary duty with the 388th Tactical Fighter Wing operating out of Korat Royal Thai Air Force Base in Thailand. Horner was going to fly combat missions over North Vietnam.

## Duty in Vietnam

In April 1965 Horner was ordered to report to Travis Air Force Base in San Francisco. The orders did not stipulate why, but as soon as he arrived in California he knew he was headed to a war zone. Horner received an empty bag, then a number of items that could only be necessary for combat—a rifle, mosquito netting, pistol, and other necessities.

Horner loved his combat experience. He flew forty-one missions against North Vietnamese supply lines, usually accompanied by at least one other aircraft. The pilots flew over enemy territory until they spotted an attractive target, dropped their bombs, and returned to safety in Thailand to plan the next day's mission.

*Horner served as a bomber pilot during his first stint in Vietnam in 1965.*

lect its best aviators, send them to war, and keep them there until the war was over. He thought that constantly rotating experienced pilots to the United States diluted the air arm's effectiveness and lengthened the war.

While serving as an instructor, Horner heard about a group of fliers called the Wild Weasels, pilots whose job in Vietnam was to fly low enough to draw the fire from North Vietnamese missile sites so that other American aircraft could learn their location and bombard the missiles. The dangerous assignment accepted volunteers only and Horner, eager to return to combat, asked to be placed with the unit.

He returned to Korat in May 1967 for a four-month stint with the Wild Weasels. Though he had frequent close calls with enemy fire, Horner accepted it as part of his job as a career pilot. During his brief stay, Horner flew another seventy missions over North Vietnam.

Like most military men of his generation, the Vietnam experience deeply affected Horner. He was a soldier whose main duty was to fight wars, but he observed too many instances where American politicians refused to let the military properly do its job. Instead of handing them the weapons and telling them to keep fighting until the war is won, politicians placed a long list of restrictions on the military. Certain airfields near North Vietnam's main city, Hanoi, were off limits to attack out of

After four months, Horner was ordered back to the United States. For two years he served at Nellis Air Force Base in Nevada as an instructor. At the time, air force superiors reasoned that experienced combat pilots would be able to impart valuable lessons to student aviators, so they pulled a large number of combat pilots out of Vietnam.

Horner did not agree with the sentiment. He believed that a nation should se-

fear that the North Vietnamese would increase their retaliation, while mounds of supplies on docks had to be avoided for similar reasons.

Horner and the other pilots reasoned that the enemy would use these tools against them anyway, and the purpose of war was to win, not to avoid antagonizing the enemy. Horner argued that the enemy was already angry with the United States—that is why the war was being fought—and that the American military should not have to worry about inciting them to further action. But they could do little about the annoying restrictions but hope they did not lose their lives because of them.

Airmen know that one of the main tenets in warfare is to gain air superiority over the enemy—to control the skies—but in Vietnam this was forbidden. Horner and other pilots simply flew over the objective, dropped their bombs, and headed back to base. This meant that each time they ventured into North Vietnam, they faced enemy fire from the same locations—spots that could have been eliminated by a coordinated attack. Politicians feared an escalation in the war, however, and declared the targets off limits.

Horner saw no overriding strategy guiding the air offensive. He claimed that this did nothing to bring victory close and only succeeded in hurting the American military. "As a result, we filled their POW [prisoner of war] camps with our pilots and littered their countryside with downed aircraft." Horner stated that the only way to wage war was to put 100 percent effort into it from the start. "If you are going to kill someone, you better have a good reason for it. And if you have a good reason, then you better not play around with the killing."[84]

Horner hated conducting warfare in such a fumbling, confused fashion and swore to avoid it in the future if he could. "I vowed if I ever got in charge, I would not let such madness reign."[85]

## In Between Wars

He would have to wait twenty-four years to make good on his vow. In the meantime Horner served in thirteen different posts over the next twenty years. He experienced a wide variety of assignments, from commanding fighter groups in the United States to formulating plans for combined air, sea, and land operations. He studied weapons systems to recommend their best possible use, and worked with other rising stars at the main military command center at the Pentagon in Washington, D.C.

By now the Horner family had expanded to five. Daughter Susan had been born during his service in England, John while Horner was at Seymour Johnson Air Force Base, and Nancy Jo while he served in Washington.

At the same time, Horner continued his education to further his military career. He earned a master's degree in business administration from the College of William and Mary in 1972 and spent more than one year at the National War College from 1975 to 1976. At each step, he impressed superiors with his command ability and tendency to quickly arrive at solutions.

The favorable reviews showed in his gradual rise through the ranks. He was promoted to lieutenant colonel in November 1973, achieved the rank of full colonel in February 1975, then made brigadier general in August 1982. Before the decade ended, Horner advanced two more grades to lieutenant general.

As he did with his time in Vietnam, Horner absorbed lessons at each step during these twenty years. From his work at the Pentagon, he learned how difficult it was in a large organization to win support for a new idea. Whenever he or an associate proposed something revolutionary, such as a

new weapons system or new ways to use older weapons systems, they received opposition from those who preferred things the way they were. New ideas usually consign old ideas to the trash heap, and those who rose to prominence under the old ideas fought tenaciously to maintain them. Horner thus had to learn the art of diplomacy—the ability to get diverse groups of individuals to work together and compromise—to achieve any success.

He also learned that a good commander does not have to lead through fear. He observed that screaming at people did nothing but antagonize. If he was dealing with a competent officer, the person already understood that they made a mistake and felt bad about it, so Horner never did more than point out the mistake and discuss how to avoid it in the future. Inferior personnel generally cared little about

*A North Vietnamese antiaircraft crew in Hanoi, North Vietnam, fires at enemy planes in 1967.*

things anyway, so Horner believed that yelling at them did no good either.

With the other military men of his time, Horner tried to instill pride in his men. He believed that the disastrous experience in Vietnam, when soldiers who returned to the United States were called "baby-killers" or were spat on, removed pride from the military. He intended to restore it by assigning clear objectives and by rewarding initiative.

"For a military person, pride is vital," stated Horner.

How else do you think we get people to work long days and weekends, leave their families at a moment's notice, endure living in tents and eating packaged food that no grocery store could sell, and do all that with minimum pay and the expectation that they might have to lay down their very lives?[86]

That pride was soon to reap dividends in the deserts of Kuwait.

## The Gulf War

When Saddam Hussein moved his forces into Kuwait, the American government organized a worldwide response that demanded that the Iraqi dictator withdraw or face military action. Horner, as commander of U.S. Central Command Air Forces, had the responsibility for supervising the use of American air power throughout the Middle East. As such, he had to assemble an effective air plan to implement against Hussein in Kuwait.

Horner took the aggressive approach that air power alone could bring Hussein to the peace table. He suggested to the chairman of the Joint Chiefs of Staff, Gen. Colin Powell, and to his immediate superior, the commander in chief of the U.S. Central Command, Gen. H. Norman Schwarzkopf, that his aircraft bomb downtown Iraq, where many Iraqi military leaders were, as well as crucial military targets and other important communications centers throughout the nation. He believed that a punishing air assault would disrupt supply and com-munications lines with the Iraqi troops in Kuwait and diminish their desire to fight.

"The Air Force believed that they could leap over the army of occupation that Saddam had in Kuwait and the related forces in southern Iraq to strike at the heart of Iraqi power," explained military analyst Rick Atkinson. "They believed that there were certain centers of gravity which would cause the Iraqi regime to buckle and perhaps to topple that didn't involve going out and taking out every artillery tube or every Iraqi tank."[87]

Horner commanded a mighty arsenal with which to implement the attack. More than 1,800 American fighters and bombers were supported by 435 additional aircraft from Saudi Arabia, Great Britain, and France.

## Horner Holds On

General Horner faced a trying time in Saudi Arabia. He commanded the nucleus of what would become a potent American presence, but until the forces poured into the region he had to hold on with what he had. Michael R. Gordon and Bernard E. Trainor explain the predicament in their analysis of the Gulf War, *The Generals' War.*

Every day, Horner spent his time trying to make arrangements to "bed down" the steady stream of aircraft headed to the Gulf and keep up the flow of ground forces to the Saudi kingdom. Every night he went to sleep thinking about what he would do if the Republican Guard drove south into the oil-rich Eastern province of Saudi Arabia.

*Horner commanded the air arm of the U.S. forces, which included over eighteen hundred fighters and bombers.*

However, both Powell and Schwarzkopf were skeptical that air power on its own could bring down Hussein. They were convinced that a ground attack would also be necessary and that to make the ground assault effective they needed support from air force bombers against battlefield targets. In their opinion, Horner's plan ignored these targets.

In effect, Schwarzkopf "blew up and he told both Horner and the chief Air Force planner, a man by the name of Glosson, 'If you people won't do it, I'll fire you and get somebody who will,'"[88] said military historian Bernard Trainor. Faced with the wrath

of his commanding officer, Horner adjusted the air plan to include targets closer to American troops.

Horner wondered if he would experience the same ineffective political leadership which haunted him in Vietnam, but his first meeting with President George Bush dispelled his doubts. On August 4, 1990, he met at the presidential retreat at Camp David with Bush, Secretary of Defense Richard Cheney, and other government leaders. He closely scrutinized the president for any signs of weakness but saw none. Horner figured that since Bush had been in the navy and had been shot at, he knew the workings of the military. Bush's insistence on clearly stating the aim of intervention in Saudi Arabia was a refreshing change from the duplicity he had found in his Vietnam days.

While Schwarzkopf remained in the United States to organize what would become a massive infusion of American troops and supplies into the Middle East, Horner received temporary command of American forces already in Saudi Arabia. At that time, some observers worried that Hussein held ambitions to seize Saudi Arabia, and Horner knew that the paltry number of Americans currently on station would be ineffective against an Iraqi attack. In such an event Horner—who commanded two armored-car companies of Saudi Arabian troops and a few Americans against twenty-four Iraqi divisions—planned to delay the enemy as long as possible, fall back and regroup for a second delaying action, and continue in that fashion. At the same time American aircraft would hit Iraqi supply lines in an attempt to bring the invasion to a standstill. In the meantime, Horner waited and prayed that he had enough time to rush the slowly increasing numbers of American soldiers into the field as quickly as they arrived in Saudi Arabia.

One anecdote tells how dangerous the situation was in those August and September days. He asked one of his top assistants,

Lt. Gen. John Yeosock, what he had to repel an Iraqi attack. Yeosock pulled out a penknife, opened the blade, and muttered, "That's it."[89]

As commander in Saudi Arabia, Horner delegated much of his authority to subordinates, but he retained control in four areas. He believed that an effective commander had to adequately plan the offensive, make sure his troops were always prepared to fight, be conscious of the needs of troops, and be sensitive to troop morale by visiting the men and women in the field as much as possible. When a unit arrived from the United States, Horner tried to make an appearance as soon after as possible.

He made two important decisions that affected his troops. Since the American forces were stationed in Saudi Arabia, a nation which still viewed women as second-class citizens, relations with the host nation were difficult. The Saudis worried that female American soldiers would drive in public or do tasks they considered fit only for men. When Saudi officials asked Horner to remove women from combat areas, he refused. While he promised to do his best to create smooth relations, he reminded the Saudis that "these women will be leaving their homes, and in many cases their children, to come to the aid of your nation. Some of them may very well shed their blood, give up their lives in the defense of the Kingdom."[90]

When his own superiors suggested that he rotate his air force pilots so that no one would remain in the theater of operation long, Horner bristled. He had seen the inefficiency of that step in Vietnam and refused to let it happen again. He answered that his pilots would remain in the Middle East until war's end, and then they could go home.

Horner actually determined when the hostilities would begin. When Hussein had not withdrawn from Kuwait by the January 15, 1991 deadline, Bush ordered the military to strike as soon as possible. Schwarzkopf asked Horner when he could implement his air strikes, and Horner replied that he preferred early in the morning of January 17. That date had the least amount of moonlight and would enable American aircraft to fly toward their destinations in darkness.

On that date waves of fighters and bombers hit targets in Baghdad and other locations throughout Iraq in an attempt to gain air superiority, something the United States had never achieved over Vietnam. Though Horner and others expected heavy losses, few aircraft were shot down in the opening moments of the war. Many of Iraq's command and communications centers were destroyed, and from then on American aircraft roamed the skies with little opposition.

The American air attack appeared so successful that the press began labeling it as a video war. Images flashed across American television screens showing laser-guided missiles flying directly into their targets. At one press briefing, Horner presented reporters film of bombs heading through the open doors of a command bunker or plunging down a rooftop air shaft.

Few expected such stunning results. Within days the coalition air force ran out of important targets and switched to a secondary list. To make sure he did not forget that military success exacted a harsh price, though, the first thing Horner did every morning was check on how many aircraft had been shot down, whether the pilots were alive, and if a rescue operation had been sent.

One of the most important parts of Horner's job during the Gulf War was to hunt down and destroy Iraq's feared missiles, called Scuds. Iraq first unleashed them on January 17 against Israel, and followed the next day with attacks on Saudi Arabia. Washington quickly put pressure on Schwarzkopf to eliminate the missiles. Schwarzkopf in turn ordered Horner to handle the issue.

Horner took steps to rectify the problem. He diverted more aircraft from other targets to searching for missile sites, and he dispatched top officers to inform the Israeli government what was being done. Horner's main concern was that Israel would militarily retaliate, which could disrupt the coalition by driving Arab troops out of the alliance.

By the time the ground war commenced on February 24, most Iraqi targets had been removed by Horner's air offensive. It now remained to support the army and marine elements that moved against

Iraqi positions, which were overcome within four days.

Though some observers have criticized President Bush for halting the forces too soon and for not invading deeper into Iraq, Horner believed that the decision was proper.

> People said, "Well, if you'd just gotten Saddam Hussein, that would have solved the problem." First of all, it wouldn't have solved the problem. And think about it this way—what American or what Saudi or what Kuwaiti life is worth that of Saddam Hussein's? You're not going to fix Iraq, and so did the war end too soon? No, I don't think so."[91]

Horner later explained how the ghost of Vietnam hovered over every action that most top commanders took against Saddam Hussein.

> I think to understand the success of Desert Storm, you have to study Vietnam. That's where the lessons were learned—you don't learn from success, you learn from failure, and we had plenty of failure in Vietnam to study, things like not fighting a war decisively, things like not fully understanding the political goals.[92]

## After the War

Following his successful work in the Gulf War, Horner returned to the United States to become the commander in chief of the North American Aerospace Defense Command and United States Space Command, as well as the commander of Air Force Space Command at Peterson Air Force Base in Colorado. In this task, his final before retirement, Horner was responsible for the aerospace defense of the United States and for ensuring the favorable use of outer space for the United States.

Horner was made a full general effective July 1, 1992. Two years later, in September 1994, he retired from the air force after a distinguished thirty-six year career. He and Mary Jo moved to Shalimar, Florida, where Horner continued to be involved in military matters by writing, speaking, and consulting.

# ☆ Notes ☆

## Introduction

1. Quoted in Doris Kearns Goodwin, *No Ordinary Time*. New York: Simon & Schuster, 1994, p. 46.

## Chapter 1: George Bush: Commander in Chief

2. Quoted in *Biography Today*. Detroit: Omnigraphics, 1992, p. 2.
3. Quoted in *Biography Today*, p. 2.
4. Quoted in Herbert S. Parmet, *George Bush: The Life of a Lone Star Yankee*. New York: Scribner, 1997, p. 36.
5. Quoted in Parmet, *George Bush*, p. 37.
6. George Bush, *All the Best, George Bush: My Life in Letters and Other Writings*. New York: Scribner, 1999, p. 25.
7. Barbara Bush, *Barbara Bush: A Memoir*. New York: St. Martin's Paperbacks, 1994, p. 47.
8. Quoted in Parmet, *George Bush*, p. 119.
9. Colin L. Powell, *My American Journey*. New York: Random House, 1995, p. 387.
10. Bush, *Barbara Bush*, p. 343.
11. Quoted in Hugh Sidey, "Washington's Calmest Man," *Time*, January 28, 1991, p. 1.
12. Bush, *All the Best*, p. 496.
13. Bush, *All the Best*, p. 499.
14. Quoted in Strobe Talbott, "A Storm Erupts," *Time*, January 28, 1991, p. 2.
15. Bush, *All the Best*, p. 489.
16. Quoted in Powell, *My American Journey*, p. 522.
17. Public Broadcasting System, "Interview with Margaret Thatcher," *Frontline*, p. 12.
18. Stanley W. Cloud, "The Home Front: Exorcising an Old Demon," *Time*, March 11, 1991, p. 1.
19. Public Broadcasting System, "Interview with Rick Atkinson," *Frontline*, p. 57.
20. George W. Bush, *A Charge to Keep*. New York: William Morrow, 1999, p. 5.

## Chapter 2: Saddam Hussein: Mideast Revolutionary

21. Quoted in Michael Kelly, *Martyrs' Day: Chronicle of a Small War*. New York: Vintage Books, 1994, p. 29.
22. Quoted in Bob Woodward, *The Commanders*. New York: Simon & Schuster, 1991, p. 257.
23. Quoted in Lance Morrow, "Saddam and the Arabs," *Time*, January 28, 1991, p. 1.
24. Powell, *My American Journey*, p. 459.
25. Quoted in Woodward, *The Commanders*, p. 216.
26. Quoted in H. Norman Schwarzkopf, *It Doesn't Take a Hero*. New York: Bantam Books, 1992, p. 368.

27. Quoted in Latif Yahia and Karl Wendl, *I Was Saddam's Son*. New York: Arcade, 1997, p. 237.
28. Quoted in George J. Church, "Saddam's Options," *Time*, January 21, 1991, p. 5.
29. Quoted in Nancy Gibbs, "The Home Front," *Time*, January 28, 1991, p. 4.
30. Public Broadcasting System, "Interview with Brent Scowcroft," *Frontline*, p. 26.

## Chapter 3: Richard Cheney: Civilian Warrior

31. Quoted in "Dick Cheney," *Newsmakers 1991*. Detroit: Gale Group, 1991, p. 1.
32. Quoted in "Dick Cheney," *Newsmakers 1991*, p. 1.
33. Quoted in "Richard B. Cheney," *Current Biography Yearbook 1989*. New York: H. W. Wilson, 1989, p. 1.
34. Quoted in "Dick Cheney," *Newsmakers 1991*, p. 2.
35. Quoted in "Dick Cheney," *Newsmakers 1991*, p. 2.
36. Quoted in "Dick Cheney," *Newsmakers 1991*, p. 2.
37. Powell, *My American Journey*, p. 328.
38. Bush, *All the Best*, p. 416.
39. Quoted in Woodward, *The Commanders*, pp. 69–70.
40. Powell, *My American Journey*, p. 405.
41. Powell, *My American Journey*, p. 429.
42. Quoted in Michael R. Gordon and Bernard E. Trainor, *The Generals' War: The Inside Story of the Conflict in the Gulf*. Boston: Little, Brown, 1995, p. 141.
43. Quoted in Gordon and Trainor, *The Generals' War*, p. 141.
44. Quoted in Schwarzkopf, *It Doesn't Take a Hero*, p. 354.
45. Public Broadcasting System, "Interview with Richard Cheney," *Frontline*, p. 14.
46. Public Broadcasting System, "Interview with Richard Cheney," p. 15.
47. Public Broadcasting System, "Interview with Richard Cheney," p. 18.

## Chapter 4: Tariq Aziz: Iraq's Promoter

48. Public Broadcasting System, "Interview with Tariq Aziz," *Frontline*, p. 5.
49. Quoted in "Tariq Aziz," *Current Biography Yearbook 1991*, p. 3.
50. Public Broadcasting System, "Interview with Tariq Aziz," p. 11.
51. Public Broadcasting System, "Interview with Tariq Aziz," p. 8.
52. Quoted in Gordon and Trainor, *The Generals' War*, p. 197.
53. Public Broadcasting System, "Interview with Tariq Aziz," p. 11.
54. Quoted in Gordon and Trainor, *The Generals' War*, p. 198.
55. Quoted in George J. Church, "The Battleground: Marching to a Conclusion," *Time*, March 4, 1991, p. 7.
56. Quoted in "Tariq Aziz," *Current Biography Yearbook 1991*, p. 1.
57. Public Broadcasting System, "Interview with Tariq Aziz," p. 19.

## Chapter 5: Colin Powell: Promoter of the Military

58. Quoted in Steven V. Roberts, "What Next, Colin Powell?" *U.S. News & World Report*, March 18, 1991, p. 7.

59. Powell, *My American Journey*, p. 26.

60. Quoted in Howard Means, *Colin Powell*. New York: Donald I. Fine, 1992, p. 109.

61. Powell, *My American Journey*, p. 62.

62. Quoted in David Roth, *Sacred Honor: A Biography of Colin Powell*. San Francisco: HarperCollins, 1993, p. 99.

63. Public Broadcasting System, "Interview with Richard Cheney," p. 26.

64. Powell, *My American Journey*, p. 490.

65. Powell, *My American Journey*, p. 487.

66. Quoted in Brian Duffy, "The Right Stuff," *U.S. News & World Report*, February 4, 1991, pp. 1–2.

67. Powell, *My American Journey*, p. 609.

## Chapter 6: H. Norman Schwarzkopf: Commander

68. Schwarzkopf, *It Doesn't Take a Hero*, p. 2.

69. Quoted in Schwarzkopf, *It Doesn't Take a Hero*, p. 1.

70. Quoted in Jesse Birnbaum, "The Commander: Stormin' Norman on Top," *Time*, February 4, 1991, p. 3.

71. Quoted in Birnbaum, "The Commander," p. 3.

72. Quoted in "H. Norman Schwarzkopf," *Current Biography Yearbook 1991*. New York: H. W. Wilson, 1991, p. 2.

73. Schwarzkopf, *It Doesn't Take a Hero*, pp. 196–97.

74. Schwarzkopf, *It Doesn't Take a Hero*, pp. 202–203.

75. Quoted in "H. Norman Schwarzkopf," *Current Biography Yearbook 1991*, p. 3.

76. Schwarzkopf, *It Doesn't Take a Hero*, pp. 473-74.

77. Powell, *My American Journey*, p. 492.

78. Quoted in Birnbaum, "The Commander," p. 2.

79. Quoted in Bruce W. Nelan, "Military Tactics: Could Saddam Have Done Better?" *Time*, March 11, 1991, p. 1.

80. Quoted in "H. Norman Schwarzkopf," *Current Biography Yearbook 1991*, p. 4.

81. Public Broadcasting System, "Interview with Rick Atkinson," *Frontline*, p. 56.

82. Powell, *My American Journey*, p. 530.

## Chapter 7: Charles Horner: Lessons from the Past

83. Quoted in Tom Clancy with Gen. Chuck Horner (Ret.), *Every Man a Tiger*. New York: G. P. Putnam's Sons, 1999, pp. 34–35.

84. Quoted in Clancy with Horner, *Every Man a Tiger*, pp. 96–97.

85. Quoted in Clancy with Horner, *Every Man a Tiger*, p. 96.

86. Quoted in Clancy with Horner, *Every Man a Tiger*, p. 136.

87. Public Broadcasting System, "Interview with Rick Atkinson," p. 20.

88. Quoted in Gordon and Trainor, *The Generals' War*, p. 19.

89. Quoted in Clancy with Horner, *Every Man a Tiger*, p. 207.

90. Quoted in Clancy with Horner, *Every Man a Tiger*, p. 197.

91. Public Broadcasting System, "Interview with Charles Horner," *Frontline*, p. 41.

92. Public Broadcasting System, "Interview with Charles Horner," pp. 3–4.

# ★ Chronology of Events ★

**1924**
George Herbert Walker Bush is born in Milton, Massachusetts, on June 12.

**1934**
H. Norman Schwarzkopf is born in Trenton, New Jersey, on August 22.

**1936**
Tariq Aziz is born in Tell Kaif, Iraq; Charles A. Horner is born in Davenport, Iowa, on October 19.

**1937**
Colin Powell is born in New York City on April 5; Saddam Hussein is born in Tikrit, Iraq, on April 28.

**1941**
Richard Cheney is born in Lincoln, Nebraska, on January 30.

**1942**
George Bush enlists in the navy in June.

**1944**
George Bush is shot down and rescued during a September mission in the Pacific.

**1959**
Saddam Hussein participates in an unsuccessful October assassination attempt directed against Abdul Karim Kassem and flees to Egypt.

**1962**
Colin Powell begins his first tour of duty in Vietnam in December.

**1964**
Saddam Hussein is arrested in September and spends two years in jail for his involvement in another unsuccessful assassination plot.

**1965**
Norman Schwarzkopf serves his first tour of duty in Vietnam; Charles Horner serves his first tour of duty in Vietnam.

**1966**
George Bush wins a seat in the House of Representatives.

**1967**
Charles Horner begins his second tour of duty in Vietnam in May.

**1968**
Saddam Hussein rises to power after a July coup; Tariq Aziz is named editor of the ruling Iraqi Baath Party newspaper; during his second tour of duty in Vietnam, Colin Powell saves the lives of four men in a November helicopter crash.

**1969**
Norman Schwarzkopf begins his second tour of duty in Vietnam in December.

## 1970

Norman Schwarzkopf risks his life to save other soldiers in a minefield in March; Richard Cheney is named a deputy White House adviser; George Bush is named ambassador to the United Nations in December.

## 1972

George Bush is named chairman of the Republican Party.

## 1974

Tariq Aziz is named to the Iraqi Cabinet as minister of information; George Bush is named chief of the Liaison Office in the People's Republic of China in October.

## 1975

Richard Cheney is named as President Gerald Ford's chief of staff.

## 1976

George Bush is named head of the Central Intelligence Agency in January.

## 1979

Richard Cheney begins his first term in the U.S. House of Representatives; Tariq Aziz is named deputy prime minister.

## 1980

Tariq Aziz escapes an assassination attempt on April 1; Aziz becomes Iraqi foreign minister; Saddam Hussein launches an invasion of Iran on September 2, starting the bloody eight-year war between the two nations.

## 1981

George Bush is sworn in as vice president.

## 1983

Norman Schwarzkopf commands all ground forces in the invasion of Grenada.

## 1986

Colin Powell is named deputy national security adviser in December.

## 1987

Charles Horner is named commander of U.S. Central Command Air Forces in March.

## 1988

The bitter Iran–Iraq war ends on July 18.

## 1989

George Bush is sworn in as president in January; Richard Cheney is approved as secretary of defense on March 17; Colin Powell is named chairman of the Joint Chiefs of Staff in October; George Bush orders soldiers to Panama to protect American interests in December.

## 1990

Saddam Hussein sends the Iraqi army into Kuwait on August 2; the United States sends the first American aircraft to the Persian Gulf on August 8.

## 1991

Tariq Aziz meets with U.S. secretary of state James Baker in Geneva on January 9; American warplanes bomb Iraqi targets on January 17, starting military action in the Gulf War; Tariq Aziz meets with Soviet Union leader Mikhail Gorbachev on February 17 and February 22; the ground war begins on February 24; military action ceases on February 28 with the Iraqi army in disarray; Tariq Aziz loses the duties as foreign minister; Norman Schwarzkopf retires from the military in August.

## 1992

Charles Horner is named commander in chief, North American Aerospace Command and U.S. Space Command in June; Horner becomes a full general in July; George Bush loses the presidential election to Arkansas governor Bill Clinton in November.

## 1993

Richard Cheney leaves government to accept a position in business; Colin Powell retires from the military in September.

## 1994

Charles Horner retires from the military in September.

## 2000

Saddam Hussein remains in power, the only one of the seven profiled individuals.

# ★ For Further Reading ★

## Books

Warren Brown, *Colin Powell.* Philadelphia: Chelsea House, 1992. Brown's book delivers decent material about Powell's career up to 1990, but it lacks depth thereafter due to insufficiency of available research material. Brown's coverage of Powell's early years in the military and his experience in Vietnam is particularly good.

*Current Biography Yearbook 1983*, S. V. "Bush, George." New York: H. W. Wilson, 1983. A good short summary of Bush's life before he became president.

Jim Haskins, *Colin Powell: A Biography.* New York: Scholastic, 1992. Haskins, a highly esteemed writer, produces an excellent short account of Powell's life intended for the upper elementary–middle school student. He uses anecdotes to enliven his book.

Don Nardo, *The Persian Gulf War.* San Diego: Lucent Books, 1991. One of the first books to appear for the teenage market about the Gulf War, Nardo does a good job summarizing the causes and basic military movements. Since the book appeared so soon after the war, Nardo is hampered by lack of information about key campaigns, but he is thorough in discussing events leading up to the war.

Rob Schneiderman, *The Picture Life of George Bush.* New York: Franklin Watts, 1989. This brief account, written for elementary students, is a decent place to start research on the life of George Bush.

Rebecca Stefoff, *George H. W. Bush.* Ada, OK: Garrett Educational Corporation, 1990. Written for the middle school market, Stefoff delivers a fine summary of Bush's life prior to the Gulf War. The book lacks enough anecdotes to breathe life into President Bush, however.

Rebecca Stefoff, *Norman Schwarzkopf.* Philadelphia: Chelsea House, 1992. The author creates a compelling biography of Schwarzkopf. Completed shortly after the Gulf War and smoothly written for junior high school students, Stefoff's book is a superb place to begin research on the general.

## Periodicals

George J. Church, "So Far, So Good," *Time,* January 28, 1991. This article provides a useful look at the opening week of fighting between the United States and Iraq.

Dan Goodgame, "Bush's Biggest Gamble," *Time,* January 28, 1991. The author presents President Bush's thoughts and attitudes during the Persian conflict and reveals how the experience in Vietnam affected Bush's actions against Saddam Hussein.

Michael Kramer, "The Moment of Truth," *Time*, January 21, 1991. A look at attitudes existing in the United States shortly before the outbreak of hostilities in the Persian Gulf.

Richard Lacayo, "A Reluctant Go-Ahead," *Time*, January 21, 1991. The author presents prevailing congressional views toward war with Hussein.

Scott MacLeon, "With His Country in Ruins, How Long Can Saddam Hang On?" *Time*, March 11, 1991. The author focuses on the damage done to the Iraqi economy and country and doubts that Hussein can survive much longer. Subsequent events proved the reporter wrong.

Carla Anne Robbins, "Top Guns of Desert Storm," *U.S. News & World Report*, February 11, 1991. Robbins presents brief profiles of the top commanders in the Gulf War. The material contains some interesting quotes.

## ✭ Works Consulted ✭

### Books

*Biography Today*. Laurie Harris, ed. Detroit: Omnigraphics, 1992. A useful introduction into George Bush's life, with strong emphasis on those who influenced him.

Barbara Bush, *Barbara Bush: A Memoir*. New York: St. Martin's Paperbacks, 1994. Mrs. Bush delivers a thorough account of her years with George Bush. Her candid comments make this a delightful book, and her account of the loss of her daughter, Robin, is especially moving.

George Bush, *All the Best, George Bush: My Life in Letters and Other Writings*. New York: Scribner, 1999. The former president uses numerous letters, diary entries, and notes to produce a loosely structured autobiography. Many relevant bits of information are scattered throughout the volume.

George W. Bush, *A Charge to Keep*. New York: William Morrow, 1999. The autobiography of George H. W. Bush's son was written in time to assist the son's presidential campaign, but it contains valuable information about the elder Bush.

Tom Clancy with Gen. Chuck Horner (Ret.), *Every Man a Tiger*. New York: G. P. Putnam's Sons, 1999. Clancy, the author of military thrillers, tells the story of Horner's life. He includes much material on Horner's time in Vietnam, how that experience affected him, and his role in the Persian Gulf War.

*Current Biography Yearbook 1991*, Charles Moritz, ed., S.V. "Aziz, Tariq." New York: H. W. Wilson, 1991. A solid, brief account of Aziz's life that is an excellent place to start in learning about Aziz.

*Current Biography Yearbook 1991*, Charles Moritz, ed., S.V. "Schwarzkopf, H. Norman." New York: H. W. Wilson, 1991. A solid account of Schwarzkopf's career.

*Current Biography Yearbook 1989*, Charles Moritz, ed., S.V. "Cheney, Richard B." New York: H. W. Wilson, 1989. An excellent brief summary of Cheney's life that was written before the war with Iraq. It gives useful information on his start in politics.

*Current Biography Yearbook 1981*, Charles Moritz, ed., S.V. "Hussein, Saddam." New York: H. W. Wilson, 1981. A superb survey of Hussein's life based on published newspaper and magazine articles.

*Encyclopedia of World Biography*, S.V. "Cheney, Richard B." Detroit: Gale Research, 1998. Another superb summary of Cheney's life that includes relevant quotes as well as information about the war with Iraq.

Doris Kearns Goodwin, *No Ordinary Time.* New York: Simon & Schuster, 1994. A superb account of Franklin and Eleanor Roosevelt during World War II. The writer uses numerous anecdotes and quotes from letters to breathe life into the couple's lives.

Michael R. Gordon and Bernard E. Trainor, *The Generals' War: The Inside Story of the Conflict in the Gulf.* Boston: Little, Brown, 1995. Military correspondent Gordon and retired Marine Corps lieutenant general Trainor combine to deliver a thoughtful analysis of the Gulf War. Their emphasis is obviously on the military aspects of the situation.

Michael Kelly, *Martyrs' Day: Chronicle of a Small War.* New York: Vintage Books, 1994. News reporter Kelly writes his memoirs of his time in the Middle East during the Gulf War. He includes valuable material on what it was like in Iraq and how the Iraqi citizen viewed events.

Howard Means, *Colin Powell.* New York: Donald I. Fine, 1992. Howard Means, a respected news reporter, interviewed many Powell associates to produce this biography of the general. Numerous anecdotes fill the pages, but the writing is not the smoothest.

*Newsmakers 1991.* Detroit: Gale Group, 1991. Includes a helpful account of Cheney's life from his birth to his time as secretary of defense.

Herbert S. Parmet, *George Bush: The Life of a Lone Star Yankee.* New York: Scribner, 1997. Veteran political writer and biographer Parmet delivers a readable and intelligent book about George Bush.

Colin L. Powell, *My American Journey.* New York: Random House, 1995. The general's autobiography is filled with fascinating glimpses of his life in the military and in Washington politics. The reader comes away with a solid understanding of the character and personality behind the man.

David Roth, *Sacred Honor: A Biography of Colin Powell.* San Francisco: HarperCollins, 1993. Written by a former Powell aide, this book contains some useful material. The book's poor writing and editing hurt the overall impact.

H. Norman Schwarzkopf, *It Doesn't Take a Hero.* New York: Bantam Books, 1992. Schwarzkopf's autobiography is indispensable for understanding the Gulf conflict and the struggles he faced with political superiors. The book also contains helpful material on his earlier career.

Bob Woodward, *The Commanders.* New York: Simon & Schuster, 1991. The veteran newspaper reporter, famous for breaking the story of Watergate in the 1970s, explains how the government operates during military crises. Relying on numerous interviews of key participants, Woodward fashions a readable, compelling look into Washington politics.

Latif Yahia and Karl Wendl, *I Was Saddam's Son*. New York: Arcade, 1997. The authors relate the incredible story of a man who was hired by Saddam Hussein to double as the leader's son. The book contains helpful material on what Hussein is like as a ruler.

## Periodicals

Jesse Birnbaum, "The Commander: Stormin' Norman on Top," *Time*, February 4, 1991. A fine short profile of Norman Schwarzkopf.

George J. Church, "The Battleground: Marching to a Conclusion," *Time*, March 4, 1991. The reporter gives a decent brief survey of diplomatic moves as the ground war neared.

George J. Church, "Saddam's Options," *Time*, January 21, 1991. The author reviews various courses of action Hussein could have adopted in the Gulf crisis.

Stanley W. Cloud, "The Home Front: Exorcising an Old Demon," *Time*, March 11, 1991. The reporter explains how the performance in Kuwait helped remove the bitter taste left from the debacle in Vietnam.

Brian Duffy, "The Right Stuff," *U.S. News & World Report*, February 4, 1991. Reporter Duffy presents short profiles of some of the Gulf War leaders.

Nancy Gibbs, "The Home Front," *Time*, January 28, 1991. The reporter records American reaction and attitudes in the opening days of the Persian conflict.

Lance Morrow, "Saddam and the Arabs," *Time*, January 28, 1991. An illuminating examination of Saddam Hussein and his influence in the Arab world.

Bruce W. Nelan, "Military Tactics: Could Saddam Have Done Better?" *Time*, March 11, 1991. The reporter examines the military errors made by Saddam Hussein during the Gulf War.

Steven V. Roberts, "What Next, Colin Powell?" *U.S. News & World Report*, March 18, 1991. A helpful examination of American military strategy.

Hugh Sidey, "Washington's Calmest Man," *Time*, January 28, 1991. Sidey looks at President Bush's actions in the early days of battle with Iraq.

Frank J. Stech, "Winning CNN Wars," *Parameters*, Autumn 1994. Stech provides an illuminating explanation of how media coverage effects strategy in warfare and how crucial to success is the emphasis on public relations.

Strobe Talbott, "A Storm Erupts," *Time*, January 28, 1991. The reporter presents actions and comments by politicians and military advisers during the Persian Gulf conflict.

## Other

Rick Atkinson Interview by Eamonn Matthews, writer and producer. *Frontline*. Public Broadcasting System, January 9, 1996. As a military analyst and historian, Atkinson provides valuable perspective on the strategies and leaders of the Gulf War. His explanations are concise and clear.

Tariq Aziz Interview by Eamonn Matthews, writer and producer. *Frontline*. Public Broadcasting System, January 9, 1996. The reader receives much helpful information from the Iraqi point of view about the Persian Gulf War. As suspected, Aziz blames the United States for causing the conflict.

Richard Cheney Interview by Eamonn Mathews, writer and producer. *Frontline*. Public Broadcasting System, January 9, 1996. The secretary of defense during the Gulf War presents his views on the war. Candid answers hand the reader valuable insights into the conduct of operations and the thinking behind top decisions.

Charles Horner Interview by Eamonn Matthews, writer and producer. *Frontline*. Public Broadcasting System, January 9, 1996. The commander of air forces during the Gulf War gives candid assessment of what went right and wrong during the conflict. The interview focuses mainly on the air war, but also contains many insightful comments about Schwarzkopf, Bush, and other leaders.

Brent Scowcroft Interview by Eamonn Matthews, writer and producer. *Frontline*. Public Broadcasting System, January 9, 1996. An important political adviser to presidents, Scowcroft provides helpful background material on most of the major figures of the Gulf War.

Margaret Thatcher Interview by Eamonn Mathews, writer and producer. *Frontline*. Public Broadcasting System, January 9, 1996. The former prime minister of England delivers hard-hitting assessments of the American politicians and generals of the Gulf War. She is especially critical of the decision to end the fighting so soon.

Bernard Trainor Interview by Eamonn Matthews, writer and producer. *Frontline*. Public Broadcasting System, January 9, 1996. As an officer, General Trainor's comments on the military and political aspects of the Gulf War have insight and value. He supplies needed information for an understanding of the conflict.

# ★ Index ★

# ✶ Picture Credits ✶

Cover photos: Center: © Wally McNamee/Corbis; Top Right: © Corbis; Bottom Right: © Corbis; Bottom Left: © AFP/Corbis; Top Left: © Francoise de Mulder/Corbis

© AFP/Corbis, 13, 16, 33

Archive Photos, 10 (top), 14, 19, 21, 29, 76

© Bettman/Corbis, 31, 37, 41 (bottom), 89, 101, 103, 105

© Corbis, 25, 82, 99, 100

© Kevin Fleming/Corbis, 78

© Bill Gentile/Corbis, 53

© George Hall/Corbis, 54

© Shel Hershorn, UT Austin/Archive Photos, 17

© Wally McNamee/Corbis, 7, 50

© Francoise de Mulder/Corbis, 59, 60, 64, 69, 92

© Caroline Penn/Corbis, 61

© Galen Powell/Corbis, 48

Reuters NewMedia/Corbis, 45, 46

Reuters/Archive Photos, 12

Reuters/Jonathan Bainbridge/Archive Photos, 86, 93

Reuters/Russell Boyce/Archive Photos, 94

Reuters/Andy Clark/Archive Photos, 97

Reuters/D.O.D./Greg Bos/Archive Photos, 107

Reuters/Stephen Jaffee/Archive Photos, 73

Reuters/Faleh Kheiber/Archive Photos, 28, 34

Reuters/Win McNamee/Archive Photos, 84

Reuters/Jacky Naegelen/Archive Photos, 41 (top)

Reuters/Fatih Saribas/Archive Photos, 43

Reuters/Bruce Young/Archive Photos, 72, 81

© David Rubinger/Corbis, 56

Arnold Sachs/CNP/Archive Photos, 11

The Smithsonian Institute, 9, 10 (bottom)

© Peter Turnley/Corbis, 66, 87

# ★ About the Author ★

John F. Wukovits is a junior high school teacher and writer from Trenton, Michigan, who specializes in history and biography. Besides biographies of Anne Frank, Jim Carrey, Stephen King, and Martin Luther King Jr. for Lucent, he has written biographies of the World War II commander Admiral Clifton Sprague, Barry Sanders, Tim Allen, Jack Nicklaus, Vince Lombardi, and Wyatt Earp. A graduate of the University of Notre Dame, Wukovits is the father of three daughters—Amy, Julie, and Karen.